CONTENTS

SECTION 1
FOUNDATIONS

SECTION 2
INTERFACE AND CONTENT

SECTION 3
DELIVERY AND SUPPORT

WEBSITE CONTENTS

The following materials are available for download from

www.wiley.com/go/bozarth

password: professional

Chapter 1

Development Checklist for Creating an e-Learning Program (pdf)

Process Overview (Bitmap image)

Chapter 3

Help: Working with Slide Masters. http://office.microsoft.com/en-us/
powerpoint-help/what-is-a-slide-master-HA102749639.aspx
(Microsoft site)

Tutorial: Action Settings Tutorial (PowerPoint files)

Tutorial: Creating GUI with Tabbed Navigation: Figure 3.24 (Windows
Media file)

Example: "Meet the Team" course intro from Tom Kuhlmann (Articulate
Player) http://articulate.www.resources.s3-website-us-east-1.ama-
zonaws.com/community/blogdemo/meetteam/player.html (note
use of hyperlinking and the cropping tool)

Chapter 9

Telephone Skills Simulation Tutorial (PowerPoint files, Windows Media files)

Chapter 10

Link to course from figure (Word document)

Appendix

Keyboard Shortcuts (Word document)

Better **Than Bullet Points**

Creating Engaging e-Learning with PowerPoint®

Second Edition

JANE BOZARTH

WILEY

Published by Wiley

One Montgomery Street, Suite 1200, San Francisco, CA 94104-4594

www.wiley.com

Cover design: JPuda

Cover image: © TUNA TIRKAZ/Getty

For additional copies/bulk purchases of this book in the U.S. please contact 800–274–4434.

Wiley books and products are available through most bookstores. To contact Wiley directly call our Customer Care Department within the U.S. at 800-274-4434, outside the U.S. at 317-572-3985, fax 317-572-4002, or visit www.wiley.com

Wiley publishes in a variety of print and electronic formats and by print-on-demand. Some material included with standard print versions of this book may not be included in e-books or in print-on-demand. If this book refers to media such as a CD or DVD that is not included in the version you purchased, you may download this material at http://booksupport.wiley.com. For more information about Wiley products, visit www.wiley.com.

Library of Congress Cataloging-in-Publication Data

Bozarth, Jane.
  Better than bullet points: creating engaging e-learning with PowerPoint®/Jane Bozarth.—Second edition.
    pages cm
  Includes bibliographical references and index.
  ISBN 978-1-118-67427-7 (pbk.)   ISBN 978-1-118-67424-6 (ebk) -- ISBN 978-1-118-67416-1 (ebk)
  1. Employees—Training of—Computer-assisted instruction.   2. Computer-assisted instruction.   3. Microsoft PowerPoint (Computer file)   4. Presentation graphics software.   5. Internet in education.   I. Title.
  HF5549.5.T7B6196 2013
  658.3'12404028553—dc23
                                                                                        2013018081

Printed in the United States of America

PB Printing   10 9 8 7 6 5 4 3 2 1

LIST OF FIGURES AND TABLES

Chapter 3

Chapter 5

Chapter 8

ACKNOWLEDGMENTS

So it turns out that, while the first book is an exciting adventure, subsequent books are *work*. I am indebted to the dozens of people and organizations who contributed screenshots and other materials, and continue to be amazed at the remarkable and quick generosity of others. There is always danger in singling out particular entities, but I really must comment on the extraordinary help and extra effort from designer extraordinaire Kevin Thorn (www.learnnuggets.com/); Trina Rimmer (www.trinarimmer.com); the folks at http://ferl.becta.org.uk, the Royal Veterinary Cottage; Professor Danton O'Day; and Tom and Alice Atkins of Right Seat Software, makers of Vox Proxy. Many thanks to Tom Kuhlmann not only for his contributions to this book but for his remarkable contributions to the field and to his community. I am also appreciative of those who have offered feedback for this edition, particularly the instructors at colleges using it for a course textbook.

I am especially appreciative of the most generous Adam Warren of Southampton University, who contributed website materials and graciously loaned me his design for the instructional screens herein.

Thanks, too—as usual—to Wiley staff Matt Davis and Lisa Shannon (how delightful to have an editor who just gives me whatever I want!).

Because I can find no more public place to thank him, I want to mention my favorite narrator, Michael Telesca, whose good humor and patience are as valuable as his golden tones. Also, many thanks to world's best neighbor Colleen O'Connor Grochowski, Ph.D. As always, much appreciation to the world's most supportive employers, Thom Wright, Ann Gillen Cobb, and Paula Kukulinski. Thanks for letting me work.

Finally, and it is not enough: very special thanks to my dear husband Kent Underwood, who in supporting my books and The Dissertation never complained about having not eaten at our dining room table since the last millennium.

Getting the Most from This Resource

What Will This Book Do for You?

There is so much more to e-learning, and to PowerPoint®, than bullets and animated text. This book will show you how to use PowerPoint to create engaging, successful e-learning programs. This edition of *Better Than Bullet Points* updates the earlier edition to provide information on working with PowerPoint 2013, but much content is applicable to earlier versions.

Why PowerPoint?

With so many authoring tools available, why would a trainer choose to stick with PowerPoint? A better question might be, "With PowerPoint so intuitive, familiar, and easy to use, why would a trainer choose to buy an expensive authoring tool?"

- PowerPoint allows for rapid development and deployment of e-learning.

- PowerPoint provides for easy addition of graphics and simple animation.

- Many training shops have libraries of PowerPoint presentations, originally developed for classroom use, ripe for updating or rethinking as online programs.

- The advent of motion path animation gives PowerPoint users animation options previously only available to users of higher-end graphics programs.

- Even novice PowerPoint users will find the learning curve shorter than that associated with other tools (and often downplayed in the sales pitches for those tools).

- e-Learning created with PowerPoint brings with it none of the licensing fees or per-user costs associated with other tools.

- Those new to e-learning may be unaware of the time and costs attached to updating online training content; using PowerPoint can make maintenance much easier.

- And odds are, if you're a trainer, you already own PowerPoint.

Really, you may find that you never need much more for creating engaging, compelling e-learning.

According to Brian Chapman of Brandon Hall Research (2005), PowerPoint is the most popular e-learning tool on the market. Used by itself or in conjunction with a PowerPoint-based add-on authoring tool (such as Articulate Presenter), PowerPoint is being used for e-learning purposes by many small firms as well as large organizations like Nestle,

John Deere, the State of North Carolina, Deloitte Touche Tohmatsu, the American Society for Prevention of Cruelty to Animals, and Dade Behring.

Who This Book Is For

This book is primarily for the trainer wearing several hats, including that of instructional designer and, now, e-learning expert. As many readers are likely making the shift from classroom to online training approaches, there is a good deal of coverage on instructional design for e-learning. The book is intended for those with minimal (or who have no interest in) programming and coding skills, who wish to use PowerPoint partly due to its user-friendly, programming-free capabilities.

What This Book Covers

This book is not about how to use PowerPoint. It's about how to use PowerPoint's features—like animation and hyperlinking—to create good online instruction. After a decade as a classroom trainer, I returned to graduate school and, on completing a degree with a major in technology in training, set out to implement a new statewide e-learning initiative. Shocked at both the ineffectiveness and outrageous expenses associated with the e-learning programs available then, my goal was to develop sound, cost-effective approaches to online training. I found, more often than not, that PowerPoint was my tool of choice and that nearly all good online training programs I encountered used approaches easily replicable with PowerPoint. After years of providing workshops on creating good e-learning, particularly with PowerPoint, and working with participants on their own solutions, I want to make this information accessible to a broader audience: you. You've probably created (and seen) plenty of PowerPoint shows that consist mostly of bulleted text supplemented by some clip art and some simple animation. But have you ever considered using PowerPoint to create an online art history course designed to look like a *noir* mystery movie? An online interactive simulation featuring audio clips of angry customers? A "Hollywood Squares"–type game with characters based on your organization's top managers? You can do all this, and much more, with nothing more than PowerPoint.

Throughout the book I frequently repeat my mantra, "It's about design, not software," and offer many examples of ways to make online content more interesting and engaging. These are "real" examples, found from web searching or from submissions from workshop participants. They were chosen for inclusion here due to their unique approach, unusual treatment, or especially compelling use of material. Even though all were not necessarily developed with PowerPoint, they all use approaches that could be replicated with PowerPoint. This book will help you see how to do that.

A suggestion: look at as many e-learning programs as you can. Search www.google.com for "e-learning showcase," "e-learning demo," "e-learning samples," and "e-learning gallery." (See especially samples at Cathy Moore's site http://blog.cathy-moore.com/resources/elearning-samples/) Also try substituting "distance learning" and "online learning" in the search phrases. When you see something you especially like, ask, "How did they do that? Can I do that?" and "Can I do that with PowerPoint?" Often the answer will be, "Yes!"

Things to Look for

Watch for the "Lesson Learned" boxes for tips on saving time, energy, and frustration, These are all things that I, or a colleague, learned the hard way. Look, too, for the website icon, shown in the margin here.

The website for this book provides printable tools, some quick tutorials, and examples of working animations and interactions described in the book, along with instructions for creating them. As site addresses and products are prone to change, and as new products are always being launched, I often suggest searching the Internet for additional information or ideas. The "search" icon indicates search terms to help guide you; with most searches, while you may end up with hundreds of hits, pay most attention to the first few pages.

Note: This book includes dozens of screenshots taken from e-learning programs. For the sake of clarity, and to ensure images would print clearly, these have sometimes been modified from their original form. Often the example has been stripped of additional elements like logos, template features, textured backgrounds, and so forth, so that it appears in "bare bones" form. Other times changes have been made to color, particularly gradient or shaded colors, to ensure that the images would print correctly in black and white for use in this book. In most cases the examples shown are accompanied by links to the original programs so that you can see them in their entirety and in their original format. See also the "Other Resources" section at the end of the book.

Technology Skills

This book was written for the trainer or instructional designer who has basic PowerPoint skills. If you can create a simple slide show, add and resize clip art and photographs, make some use of Word Art, and know how to make a line of text fly in, then this book should be appropriate for you. The Appendix provides a quick overview of PowerPoint tools. Those with very rudimentary skills might want to practice basic tasks or seek out additional training.

Searching www.google.com for specific tasks, such as "how to create animations in PowerPoint," will take you to any number of tutorials.

While this is not a "how to use PowerPoint" text, I have in some cases included step-by-step instructions for several operations. Decisions about when to do this were driven by questions I most frequently receive during workshops or during consultations. Most often, questions arise not from how to use a particular built-in feature but how to manipulate something in a way that may not be evident. For instance, most participants understand the basics of hyperlinking, but have never considered how to use that capability to create a simulation or game-show-type game. Similarly, most people grasp the idea of simple animation—it's available through drop-down menus—but few have explored the possibilities of editing clip art. Questions also arise about functions that are beyond those typically associated with using PowerPoint for classroom presentations—for instance, adding narration or uploading to the web. Instructions have been included for these pursuits.

This new edition of *Better than Bullet Points* was designed to go to press in time with the release of PowerPoint 2013. (The first edition was aimed at those using PowerPoint 2002, 2003, and 2007.) In many cases there is little difference; where there is a variation in interface or commands I have tailored those to 2013 users. This should not cause too many problems for readers with earlier releases of PowerPoint.

How to Use This Book

As this book offers a chronological tour through the process of creating e-learning with PowerPoint, I recommend reading chapters in order, then returning to sections as need be. The book does sometimes reference material covered earlier, so familiarity with the content will help. It seems that every PowerPoint user, regardless of level, has a particular area of interest and skill. Those with an artistic bent may know a great deal about creating from-scratch illustrations, while having no experience with adding narration; others may have extensive experience with complex animations while knowing nothing about compressing images. So skim where you feel you should, but please look out for new ideas, examples, and tips even in areas where you feel you are fluent.

What This Book Covers

Chapter 1 provides an overview, with many examples, of the possibilities of using PowerPoint for developing e-learning. We then begin a chronological tour of creating good PowerPoint-based e-learning programs. Chapter 2 discusses the basics of instructional design for e-learning, with particular attention paid to setting clear goals, reducing cognitive load, and practical applications of the research on multimedia learning. This chapter also walks through the process of transforming former classroom content for online delivery and ends with ideas on choosing an appropriate treatment and examples of creating a basic program layout. Chapter 3 deals with developing a good user interface, creating navigation, and making decisions about learner control. Chapter 4 addresses the issue of choosing graphics and text that are meaningful, rather than decorative, and examines the impact the right images can have. In Chapter 5 we extend this discussion to creating and editing images for use in e-learning programs. Chapter 6 offers a look at effective animations and, as with the discussion of images, the focus is on animations that teach rather than entertain. Chapter 7 provides extensive examples of creating interactions, from quizzes and games to simulations with branching decision making. Chapter 8 provides examples of some add-ons, like animated talking characters, and discusses ways of extending programs through blended learning and collaborative experiences, and includes examples of performance support tools, job aids, and ideas for "nice to know" content. Chapter 9 covers the final step of development, adding narration and multimedia. And in Chapter 10 we look at ways of distributing our e-learning programs to our learners. The Appendix offers a quick overview of basic PowerPoint features and commands. Finally, the References and Other Resources sections are meant to provide more than just citations for material: please visit sites listed, or take a look at authors quoted, for inspiration and further education.

Disclaimer

 This book references a number of websites and particular products. There is always danger when talking about web technologies: site addresses change, companies merge, and products disappear. Please check the book site www.wiley.com/go/bozarth for updates, information about changes, or revised links.

SECTION 1

Foundations

CHAPTER 1

Creating e-Learning with PowerPoint

There's an urban myth that humans use only 2 percent of their brains. While that's never been substantiated, the idea does seem to bear out in regard to PowerPoint: most users employ just a fraction of PowerPoint's capabilities. Those of us in training know that an awful lot of classroom PowerPoint shows are just mind-numbing screen after screen of bulleted text. Adventuresome trainers may add some decorative elements like spinning slide transitions, pretty clip art, or animated text. In its worst application, poorly designed PowerPoint shows are uploaded to the web and called "e-learning." But they aren't "e-learning" programs. They are e-presentations or e-lectures or e-reading, but there's no learning there any-where. Likewise, those who think PowerPoint can't be used to create good e-learning programs have likely only seen PowerPoint at its worst: slide after slide of bulleted lists, dizzying irrelevant animation, and decorative rather than meaningful graphics. (For that matter, many e-learning programs, regardless of the authoring tool used, suffer from the same problems. Search Google for a common topic like "online safety training" and see what you find.)

> In user testing, Microsoft found that nine out of every ten features
> that customer wanted to see added to Office products were already
> in the program.
>
> **Ina Fried, www.CNEDnews.com, September 2005**

It's a shame that PowerPoint is so often badly used or underused
because it can be so much more than a presentation tool. For those
interested in e-learning, it can often replicate what is otherwise done
with expensive authoring tools. With PowerPoint, some imagination,
and some patience, you can create interesting, engaging online courses
with meaningful interactivity. Figures 1.1 through 1.7 show some
examples of PowerPoint's potential.

Examples

Multiple-Choice Quizzes

Figure 1.1. Multiple-Choice Quiz

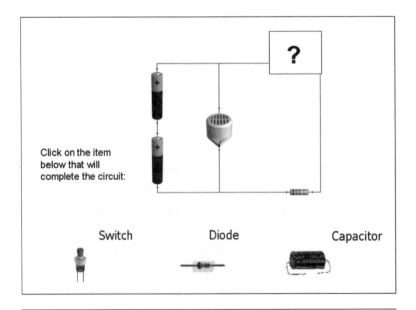

Source: Simon Drane. Component images. www.crocodile-clips.com

Matching Exercises

Figure 1.2. Matching Exercise

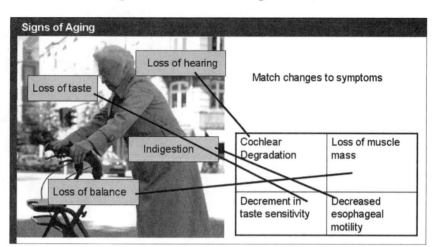

Game-Show-Type Quiz

Figure 1.3. Jeopardy-Type Quiz

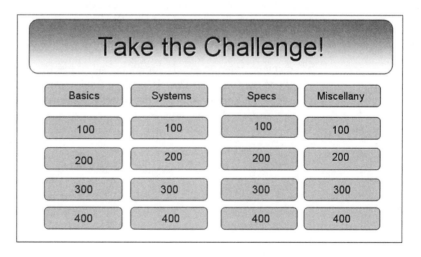

Mazes

Figure 1.4. Maze

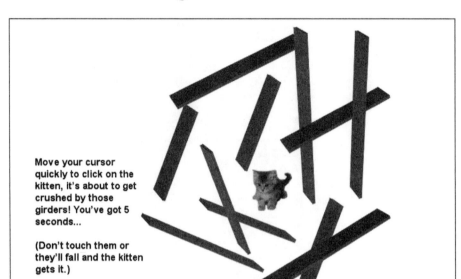

Case Studies

Figure 1.5. Case Study

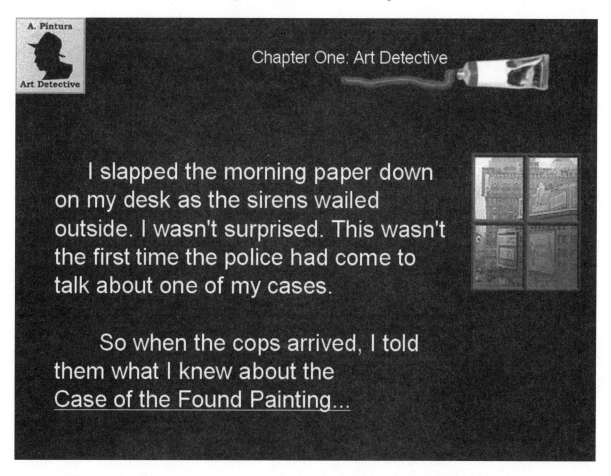

Simulations with Branching Decision Making, with
Embedded Audio and Video Clips

Figure 1.6. Simulation with Branching Decision Making

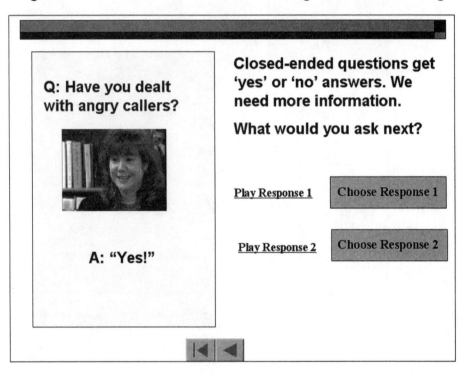

Animations That Teach

Figure 1.7. Animation Illustrating Concept

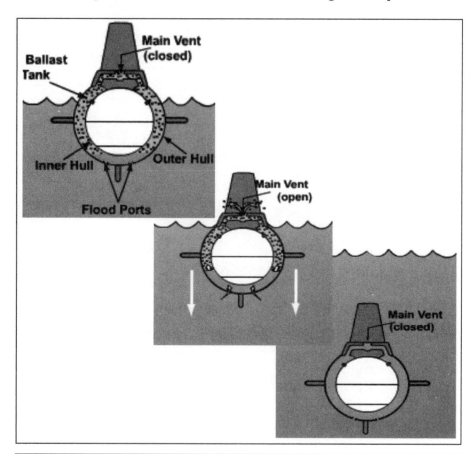

Source: www.onr.navy/mil

Let's Get Started

The rest of this book takes you on a step-by-step walk through the process of developing e-learning with PowerPoint. The chart below provides an overview of the basic process for creating an e-learning program with PowerPoint, while Table 1.1 offers a checklist (there's a printable version on the website for this book) of the process in more detail.

Chart 1.1. Process Overview

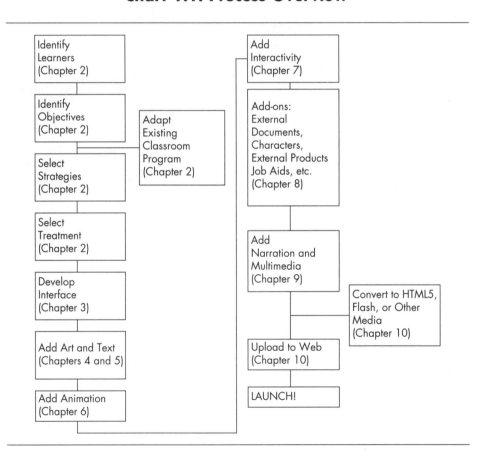

Table 1.1. Development Checklist

- ❑ Identify your learners.
- ❑ Determine objectives.
- ❑ Adapt existing classroom program (if applicable).
- ❑ Choose strategies.
- ❑ Choose treatment.
- ❑ Create main file folder and subfolders for images, media, etc.
- ❑ Develop the storyboard.
- ❑ Create graphic user interface (GUI) and slide and title masters.
- ❑ Include "how to use this program" information for new learners.
- ❑ Add art and text.
- ❑ Add animation.
- ❑ Add interactivity.
- ❑ Add narration and multimedia.
- ❑ Save everything!
- ❑ Add other elements: documents, characters, external quizzes and sites, pre- and post-work, "blended" components, job aids
- ❑ Add a site map
- ❑ Save everything!
- ❑ Convert to Flash, HTML5, MP4, or other medium (optional).
- ❑ Upload to web or LMS.
- ❑ Test.
- ❑ Launch.

The website offers narrated explanations, "you try" tutorials, examples of items like working animations and interactions, and templates for game design.

Versions

Many basics of PowerPoint have remained the same over time. Perhaps the biggest change came with the release of PowerPoint 2007, which introduced the new "ribbon" interface. Even this meant finding the new locations for familiar tools, rather than learning all the commands from scratch. PowerPoint 2010 brought some changes to authoring and version control, ability to export as a WMV video file, easy means of inserting a video with player controls, a change in how audio was edited, and a few enhancements to art capabilities.

The biggest visible change to PowerPoint 2013 is the new default widescreen 16:9 ratio, shown in Figure 1.8. It's more appropriate for newer laptops and many devices, thus creating slides now more rectangular than square (At this time, though, the old 4:3 format still ideally fits the iPad.).

Figure 1.8. New 16:9 Default Screen Ratio in PowerPoint 2013

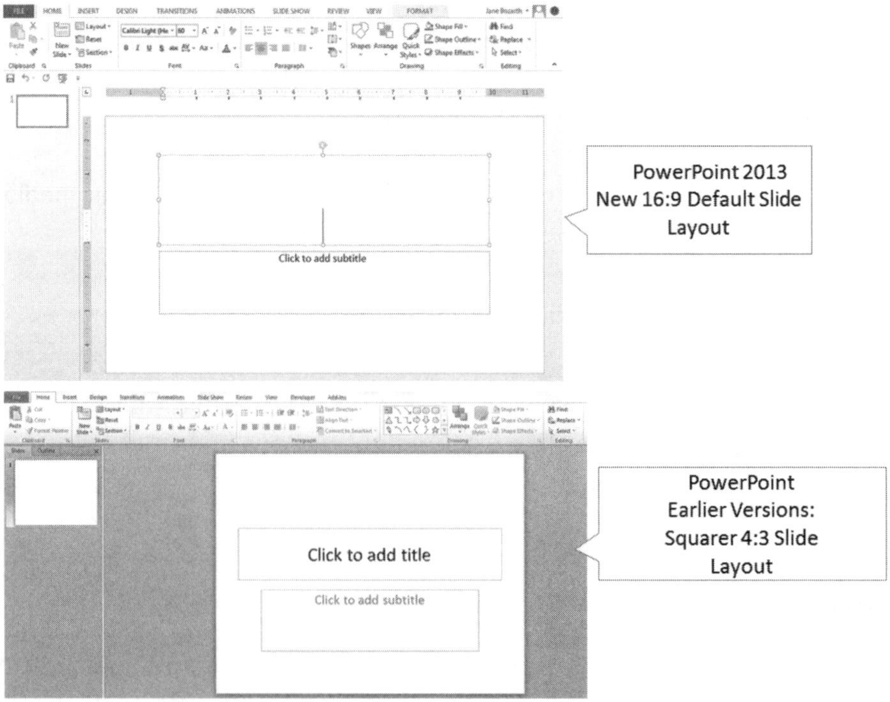

While this change makes sense, it's going to bring challenges to PowerPoint users. For one thing, old slides won't just "work" as they usually do across other versions of PowerPoint. Importing old presentations will result in a stretched look as images, text, and background are pulled to fit the rectangular frame. You can reset the slide to the old format by clicking the "Design" tab and choosing "Slide Size," but even then the transfer won't be perfect. As PowerPoint 2013 is brand-new, help on this is evolving, so search the Internet for updates and pointers. While this is going to prove challenging, it does bring increased slide space and the opportunity to do new, creative things with our projects (NOT just add more filler, though!), so try to see it as an opportunity to improve your work.

PowerPoint 2013 has added more "social" functionality, with commenting, simultaneous reviewing, and the sharing made available through SkyDrive cloud storage and sending files to SharePoint. PowerPoint 2013 is also more device-friendly, making it easier to work with on tablets and handheld devices, and the widescreen display is better suited to most newer laptops and monitors. There's also the new eyedropper color-picker tool, functionality for inserting images and videos from the web and taking screenshots, improvements in charting, and some changes in the interface.

PowerPoint 2013 allows for more sophisticated animations and makes the motion path animations more precise, and new Smart Guides help with aligning objects. There's also new capability for exporting files as MP4s, which will play on tablets and other devices.

Other things have been taken away. Windows no longer comes with the Sound Editor tool, and narration can only be recorded directly to PowerPoint in a low-quality format with some editing functionality. Better audio quality therefore now requires an add-on. It's not impossible to manage, but it's hard to understand why the tool was removed. The easy tool for swapping colors in clipart is also gone. The color swap can still be done, but it now requires ungrouping the picture and recoloring (often tiny) pieces one at a time. The updated animation pane offers something akin to a scrub bar that makes it easier to work with/preview long animations.

There's a new Start screen that offers more options for where to begin, and there's more effort to add collaboration/sharing tools and allow for cloud-based SkyDrive storage and sharing. The "File" menu, now called the "backstage" has its own screen, which expands earlier capability (see Figure 1.9).

Apart from software versions? Really, the field has changed. In the time since I worked on the first edition of this book in 2007, YouTube has exploded with hundreds of PowerPoint tutorials, on everything from animating a chart to working with slide masters. People like Tom Kuhlmann and his work with Articulate and, especially, his Rapid

Figure 1.9. New File Menu in PowerPoint 2013

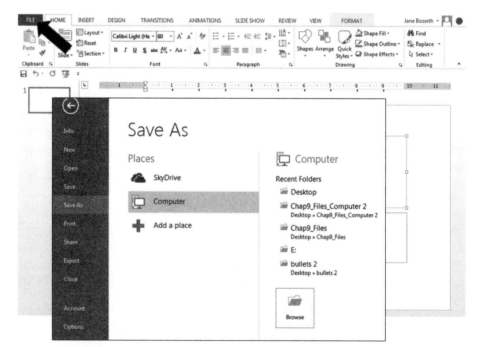

e-Learning blog have helped to further understanding of PowerPoint for e-learning design, not just presentation, and supported credibility of using PowerPoint as an authoring tool, even if it received further processing with another product.

One More Thing

Based on past readership I am assuming that readers of this edition are primarily wearing multiple hats: training practitioner, instructional designer, e-learning creator, perhaps even HR generalist or subject-matter expert. I'm also guessing that you aren't working in a huge organization with an army of programmers and designers at your disposal. For that reason I've made some choices about the examples and screenshots I provide. My goal is for you to be able to do everything described in this book and to feel confident, as you read, that you can. So sometimes, for instance, I may have chosen an example with exemplary ideas and interactions but less-than-dazzling graphics. "A. Pintura: Art Detective," an example that appears throughout the book, is not a very pretty program. But it is more effective at helping a learner learn than 95 percent of the e-learning courses I've seen. And, given a little patience, anyone with even rudimentary PowerPoint skills could re-create it. So some things here may not be as pretty or sophisticated as they could be, but they still work and they're within your reach. I hope you find everything here doable, and if you have an artistic bent—or an artist at your disposal—then by all means I hope you can improve on the basics I offer.

Next Stop: It's About Design, Not Software

This book will help you move "beyond the bullets" to new ways of thinking about PowerPoint-based e-learning. Success in applying this material isn't a matter of technical wizardry. It takes patience and creativity and a willingness to experiment and learn, as we often do, through some trial and error. I hope you enjoy this journey.

CHAPTER **2**

It's About Design, Not Software

I n breaking out of the bulleted-text box, ask: Who are your learners? What is it you're trying to accomplish, how can you do it in an engaging, effective way, and which strategies will support the goals of the training? When developing meaningful instruction, it's vital to stay focused on desired outcomes. Even those with strong skills in developing classroom-based training will find still more challenges in designing for the online environment. This chapter looks at the basics of instructional design for e-learning and offers guidelines for transforming classroom content for online delivery.

Who Are Your Learners?

Understanding your target audience will help you choose appropriate treatments and useful interactions. You cannot build credible, effective scenarios, cases, story-based experiences, and simulations without a clear understanding of your learners and their reality. What do most of them do on the job? What do the rest do? Why are they accessing this e-learning course? Is it required? By whom? What do they already know about this topic? What reactions might they have to this topic/content? Do they have a history with this topic? What is it? In approaching a new project I have a motto: "Put your hands in the air and step away from the computer." No matter what tools you end up using, it's more important that you start with ideas, not slides.

A big advantage of e-learning is "scalability", that is, a program can be delivered to many learners at once. This brings with it, though, the temptation of trying to create a program that is all things to all people, while relevant to none. Consider the issue of a company's "infection control" update. The instruction that will be effective for the general office staff will likely not be useful for the company nurses. The level of prior knowledge, tasks carried out during the work day, and expectations of performance are very different. For instance, the first group might benefit from some simple reminders about hand washing, perhaps in the form of the PowerPoint-based "Bacteriopoly" game shown in Chapter 8. Nurses, however, might need much more in-depth information. Be very clear about the needs of your target audience, and be prepared to create perhaps two levels or different versions of a program.

Objectives and Strategies

The learning objectives of your program will drive the design. What are the desired performance outcomes? It can be hard to keep these in sight when caught up in designing. And it can be challenging to develop objectives that support real-world performance. "Academic" objectives, such as, "the participant will list, define, describe. . ." are easy to write, and they're easy to teach to (lecture, bulleted slides), and they're easy to test (matching, multiple choice). But is any learning taking place that will be of any use in the workplace? My supervisor has never, ever, asked me to "list" anything.

> The problem with most learning objectives is that they "tend not to relate to anything anyone will actually be able to do in this world."
>
> **Roger Schank,** *Lessons in Training, Learning, and e-Learning*

I'm guessing that readers involved in training and instructional design have at least a passing knowledge of Benjamin Bloom's taxonomy of objectives, which describes learning in terms of level of abstraction. If you envision Bloom's ideas as a pyramid with increasingly fine points of sophistication, the lowest level, knowledge, addresses only recall and provides training that asks learners to do little more than recite a series of steps in a process or memorize some definitions of terms. The remaining climb up the pyramid would include, in order, comprehension, application, analysis, synthesis, and evaluation. (This is an extremely truncated explanation, meant as a quick reminder for those with a background with Bloom; those unfamiliar with his work are encouraged to search www.google.com for "Bloom's taxonomy.") Table 2.1 outlines levels of the taxonomy and offers ideas for strategies and activities appropriate for each.

Table 2.1. Match Outcomes to Strategies

OUTCOME if you want learner to . . .	**SOME STRATEGIES** then try . . .	**RATIONALE** because this will encourage . . .	**SPECIFICS** (and here are some ideas; all can be done online)
Knowledge List, define	Text presentation Simple test	Recall	Matching terms to definitions Ordering in correct sequence Simple multiple choice quiz Printable worksheet List the four steps in defusing an angry customer Given choices, correctly choose phrase most likely to defuse angry customer

Table 2.1. Continued

OUTCOME if you want learner to . . .	SOME STRATEGIES then try . . .	RATIONALE because this will encourage . . .	SPECIFICS (and here are some ideas; all can be done online)
Comprehend Explain, predict, describe	Restate Paraphrase Translate	Deeper understanding Connection between verbal description and behavior	Given choices, predict outcomes of different phrases in defusing angry customer Given choices, rank order phrases used to defuse angry customer, from most effective to least effective
Application Solve, experiment	Practice Determine Get a "feel" for it	Experiential learning Trial and error	Given simple scenario, utilize four-step process in defusing angry customer Given brief description of angry customer, practice using defusing phrases in a skill practice or role play
Analysis Connect, infer	Taking it apart to see how it works Isolate "precursors" to end results	Careful examination of complicated behaviors	Given complex scenario, break into component parts to identify underlying factors Given "script" of unsuccessful customer interaction, identify phrases or words that made the situation worse
Synthesis Debate, contrast, distinguish Compile, pull together, accumulate	Structured case studies Worked examples	Connect prior experience to new learning Facilitate transfer	Given complex scenario, work to identify root of customer complaint and utilize four-step process in defusing customer's anger
Evaluation Judge, choose course of action, evaluate data	Less-structured case studies, simulations	Opportunity to self-correct Provide practice Encourage reflection Facilitate transfer	Given complex less-structured scenario, generate own effective response to angry customer

Bloom further refined his thinking to include the concept of learning domains. He identified three: cognitive, psychomotor, and affective. In the training vernacular this is often restated in terms of objectives: What do you want learners to know? What do you want them to do? And how do you want them to feel? What might look like a very straightforward topic could very well include all three domains. Consider, for instance, a program on using fire extinguishers. You want the learners to know where the extinguisher is located as well as other basic fire-safety procedures. You want them to use the extinguisher correctly. And you want them to feel confident that this is a task they can handle without panicking. Other topics may involve only one domain: learning to use a new office copier very similar to the old one may involve only the psychomotor domain, while using a very different model might touch the cognitive as well as the psychomotor.

Leadership training may employ a good many strategies aimed at the cognitive and affective domains, but require little in the way of psychomotor skills. A failing of many learning programs (and live training, too, in my experience) is focusing exclusively on the cognitive domain. It's where we get hours and hours of lecture in the classroom, and screen after screen of content online. Again: Talking is easy. Presenting bullet points is easy. Figuring out how to reach the other domains—to provide psychomotor practice or to elicit an emotional response—is your challenge in developing effective PowerPoint-based e-learning.

Along with other development decisions, you will need to estimate time it will take to create your e-learning program. Here is a list of typical considerations:

- Nature of the training

- Complexity of the training

- Existing training materials (Amount/Type/Quality)

(*continued*)

- Knowledge and experience of the project manager
- Interest and attitude of the project manager
- Interest and attitude of the practice development/sales person
- Knowledge and experience of the instructional developers
- Interest and attitude of the instructional developers
- Client knowledge of development process
- Client attitude toward the project and project team
- Evaluation and pre-testing requirements and procedures
- Media elements
- Degree of learner versus system control of learning
- Materials approval process
- Number of iterations
- Development methodology
- Development and programming tools and systems
- Explicit design, development, and documentation standards
- Number and nature of mid-project changes
- Experience of the programming staff
- Experience and capabilities of the media product staff
- Requirements to interface with other systems and technology
- Existing hardware and software architecture

Thanks to Richard M. Cavagnol, Principal, Technology Applications Group, Inc.

Cognitive Load

Many e-learning programs (and many classroom PowerPoint shows, for that matter) simply ask too much of learners. The tendency toward decorative fonts, busy templates, bright background colors and textures, branding elements like company logos, and too much text, can be overwhelming. Consider the example shown in Figure 2.1, from a program someone brought to me and asked whether I would narrate, so it could be "e-learning." What is the "learning" here? There are several ideas, represented by text of equal size, with unclear connection. The template is unrelated to the content, and the graphic suggests profit rather than the productivity the text beside it mentions. It gets worse: while you can't view it here, the font of the last lines uses a blaring icy-blue shadowed text, the middle lines of text spiral and bounce while the slide loads, and every slide change is accompanied by a chiming sound effect. The learner doesn't have a chance!

Figure 2.1. Example of Cognitive Overload

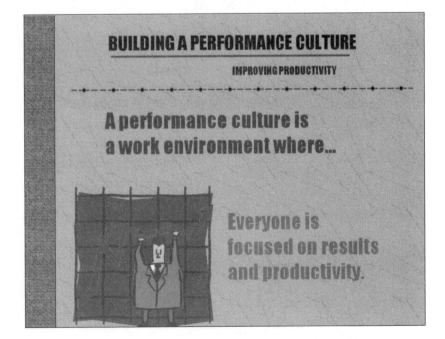

While some simple editing—cutting out extraneous information, cleaning up the look, finding more relevant graphics—could correct many of these problems, psychology professor Richard Mayer, famous for his research on multimedia learning, offers his "Select—Organize—Integrate" (SOI) model as a rubric for approaching the issue of cognitive load. How can we help learners acquire what matters? Table 2.2 offers some suggestions.

Mayer has also conducted extensive research on the effectiveness of multimedia learning (see the "References" section for studies) and has developed a number of principles useful for those of us working to

Table 2.2. Mayer's SOI Model

Select	Remove interesting but extraneous information "Chunk" information into smaller pieces Use font size, colors, and highlighting to indicate importance Be concise Use white space for emphasis
Organize	Advance organizers Graphic organizers Relevant graphics Flow charts and diagrams Process maps Steps or sequence flows
Integrate	Cases Simulations Self-assessments Elaborative questions Activities that encourage processing

develop e-learning programs. Mayer's *principles of multimedia learning* especially relevant to the purposes of this book follow:

1. *Multimedia principle:* Learning is enhanced by the presentation of words and pictures rather than words alone. Figures 2.2 and 2.3 show an example.

Figure 2.2. Before: Text List of Required Items

Written Warning

Definition:
A detailed disciplinary notice for conduct or performance

A Written Warning Must:
State that it is a warning
State the reason for the warning
Detail the improvements required
Indicate length of time allowed for improvement
State the consequences if improvements are
not made
Outline the appeal process

Figure 2.3. After: Sample Letter Shows Items in Realistic Context

MEMORANDUM
To: Jessica Jones, Office Assistant
From: Steve Smith, Office Manager
Date: October 20, 2007
Subject: Written Warning—Unsatisfactory Job Performance

The purpose of this letter is to give you written warning for unsatisfactory job performance. The specific unsatisfactory performance for which you are being warned is excessive tardiness. On August 19, September 15, and October 5 I talked with you about the importance of starting work promptly. During our last conversation we discussed the consequences of Reason rove in this area.

2. *Coherence principle:* Learning is enhanced when extraneous material is omitted. Figures 2.4 and 2.5 show another before-and-after example.

Figure 2.4. Before: Slide with Extraneous Material

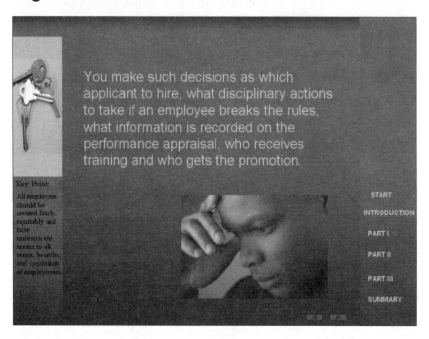

Figure 2.5. After: Slide with Extraneous Information Removed

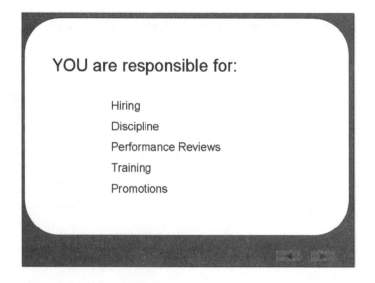

3. *Split attention principle:* This is a common problem with narrated e-learning courses. Designers add word-for-word audio voiceover to match the on-screen text. Different parts of the brain process visual and auditory information at different speeds (we usually read faster than a narrator talks); splitting attention this way causes the material to compete for the learner's attention, creates overload for the learner, and greatly reduces the learner's ability to take in the information.

4. *Redundancy principle:* Similar to the split attention principle. Mayer found that presenting animation with narration was more effective than animation plus narration and on-screen text.

5. *Contiguity principle:* Learners learn better when on-screen text and visuals are integrated rather than placed apart. The valley images shown in Figures 2.6 and 2.7 (photos used with permission of Debbie Milton) illustrate this:

Rather than ask, "How can I teach this?" ask, "How can my participants learn this?"

Nanette Miner, Ed.D., *The Accidental Trainer*

About mLearning

Changes in PowerPoint 2013, touted as improvements by many in the field and especially vendors with supplemental products, is the combination of the new 16:9 slide layout and the ability to save PowerPoint show as an MP4 file. This does mean that files will run on devices, including smart phones. That doesn't mean PowerPoint-based e-learning should be delivered this way. mLearning is its own field of

Figure 2.6. Before: Text Separated from the Image Increases Cognitive Load

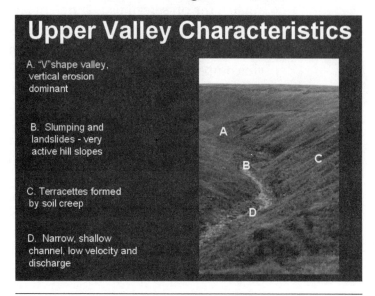

Photo used with permission of Debbie Milton

Figure 2.7. After: Text Integrated into Image Helps Learners Acquire Information

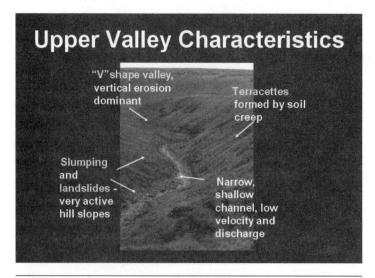

Photo used with permission of Debbie Milton

expertise with its own uses and rules. Chad Udell, author of *Learning Everywhere* (2012) offers these comments for readers of this book:

1. Good mlearning is not created via a miniaturization process of other content. It is a thoughtful, deliberate activity done in concert with the larger learning strategy. The user interface, user experiences, and use cases for mobile are so vastly different than ahead-of-time training that simply "porting" your courseware over to a mobile-friendly file format is not enough.

2. When viewed through the lens of a web or application developer's point of view, the learning industry's approach to new platforms, devices, and formats is pedestrian at best. We haven't begun to have conversations related to data interchange formats and content strategy that are a fact of life for the larger technology community. We still get hung up in the authoring and delivery runtime, neglecting to notice that is the content that makes our work valuable.

3. An easy button to create mlearning from e-learning doesn't exist. And once one does, I sincerely hope it doesn't result in a ton of bulleted, busy PowerPoint files being foisted on our learners in name of mlearning.

For more on mlearning see also Hoober and Berkman (2011) and Clark (2010).

Know what and for whom you are developing, and design accordingly—even if it means designing the same program for delivery via different devices. Regardless of the tools you may use, if it appears mobile will be a big part of your future e-learning deployment, then please pursue training in instructional design specifically for mobile delivery.

Choosing a Treatment

In developing e-learning with PowerPoint it's crucial that you consider not just developing interactivity but also ways of approaching the content. The right treatment—your overall approach—is often what moves a program from "e-presentation" to "e-learning." Bullet-ridden, content-based programs rarely get past the cognitive domain and remain at the lowest levels of Bloom's taxonomy. No authoring tool will magically create "relevant, engaging" learning on its own—and making it "pretty" doesn't make it more effective.

Figures 2.8 through 2.12 show several before-and-after examples of possible treatments.

Figure 2.8. Treatment for Program for Art Museum

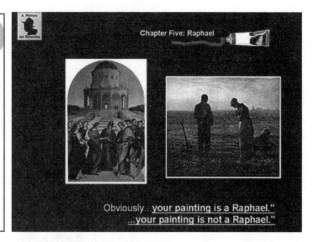

Before: List of facts

After: Interactive mystery "The Case of the Found Painting"

Source: Eduweb

Figure 2.9. Treatments for Ethics Program for New Veterinarians

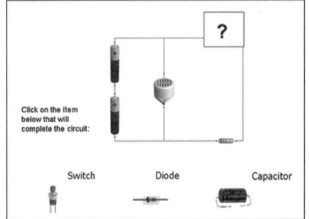

Before: List of facts   After: Interactive decision-making
                                         simulation

Source: Royal Veterinary College

Figure 2.10. Treatment for Electrical Circuitry Program

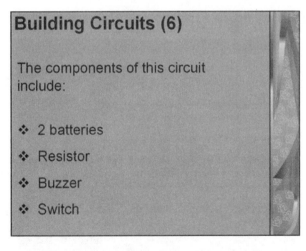

Before: Presentation of content   After: Realistic practice

Source: Simon Drane

Figure 2.11. Treatment for Sexual Harassment Course

The EAP Counselor met with the employee who had reported the situation. The employee described feelings of being overwhelmed and helpless. The demeaning remarks were becoming intolerable. The employee believed that attempts to resolve the issue with the coworker were futile. The fact that the supervisor minimized the situation further discouraged the employee. By the end of the meeting with the counselor, however, the employee was able to recognize that not saying anything was not helping and was actually allowing a bad situation to get worse.

At a subsequent meeting, the EAP counselor and the employee explored skills to address the situation in a respectful, reasonable, and responsible manner with both her supervisor and the abusive coworker. The counselor suggested using language such as:

- I don't like shouting. Please lower your voice.
- I don't like it when you put me down in front of my peers.
- It's demeaning when I am told that I am...
- I don't like it when you point your finger at me.
- I want to have a good working relationship with you.

The employee learned to focus on her personal professionalism and responsibility to establish and maintain reasonable boundaries and limits by using these types of firm and friendly "I statements," acknowledging that she heard and understood what the supervisor and coworker were saying, and repeating what she needed to communicate to them.

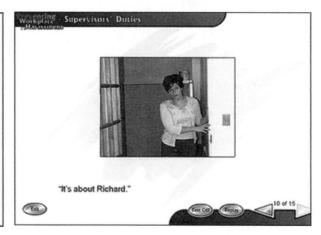

Before: "Wall of words" text content

After: Case study using photos and voice clips

Source: www.brightlinecompliance.com;HR Train/IET

Figure 2.12. Treatment for Equal Employment Opportunity Course

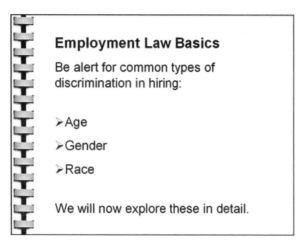

Before: Bulleted content

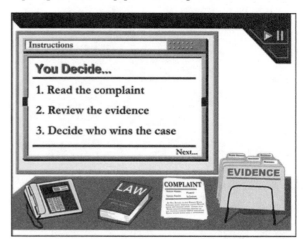

After: Interaction with elements of a case

Writer's Block?

We've just looked at various treatments for e-learning programs: a film noir mystery, a veterinary case simulation, and a job skill training practice. Finding the right approach and an interesting treatment can be challenging. There's nothing wrong with looking around to see how others have approached a topic or type of content. And brainstorming, free-writing, and free-association exercises can help. Asking someone with no knowledge at all of the topic can sometimes get you surprising suggestions for how you might approach it. Try sitting down with a blank sheet of paper and jotting down every word you can think of associated with a topic. Figure 2.13 shows a list of words I came up with when approaching on a module on the organization's complex employee discipline process. The word that popped out at me was "maze"; this ended up forming a metaphor for the treatment, a simulation that took a supervisor took an online walk through the "maze" of the process.

Figure 2.13. Free-Association

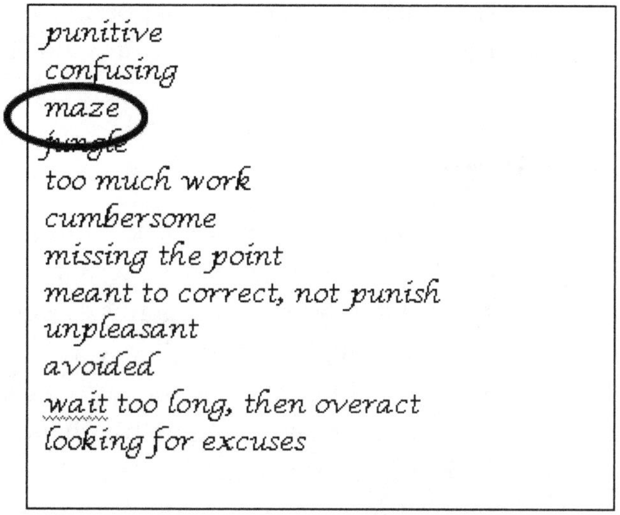

punitive
confusing
maze
~~jungle~~
too much work
cumbersome
missing the point
meant to correct, not punish
unpleasant
avoided
wait too long, then overact
looking for excuses

Source: www.eduweb.com/intura/

Table 2.3. Possible Approaches to "Sharks"

Shark: Killer of the Seas	Case of scuba diver alone battling beast Facts about how much sharks can eat an hour, how strong their jaws are, the history of terrifying attacks Learners will watch *Jaws* and write a report
Sharks are misunderstood	Video clips of children swimming with sharks Facts: great proportion of shark species no threat to humans Shark attacks very rare but get lots of press
Shark is the victim; it's man who's the killer	Facts about shark species now endangered/extinct Facts about decline

A free-writing exercise can also provide inspiration. Take a blank sheet of paper and set a timer for three minutes. Start writing, and keep writing, about the topic until the time is up. Grammar, spelling, and logic don't matter—just keep writing and see what ideas surface. Another strategy is to make a list of possible different approaches to see what treatments they might suggest. Table 3.3 provides an example.

Can You Find a Story?

Cliff Atkinson's *Beyond Bullet Points* (2005) vouches for the effectiveness of a good story to enhance presentations. Many of his ideas can be applied to e-learning programs as well. In using stories in online learning, think of good storytellers you know and good stories you've heard. You'll usually find some interesting characters, a problem to be handled, and a resolution—often with a "happy ending." In online programs such stories often take the form of case studies or simulations, such as the art history mysteries of "A. Pintura: Art Detective" (Figure 2.14) and the impossible decisions faced by the characters struggling for survival

Figure 2.14. Story: "A. Pintura: Art Detective"

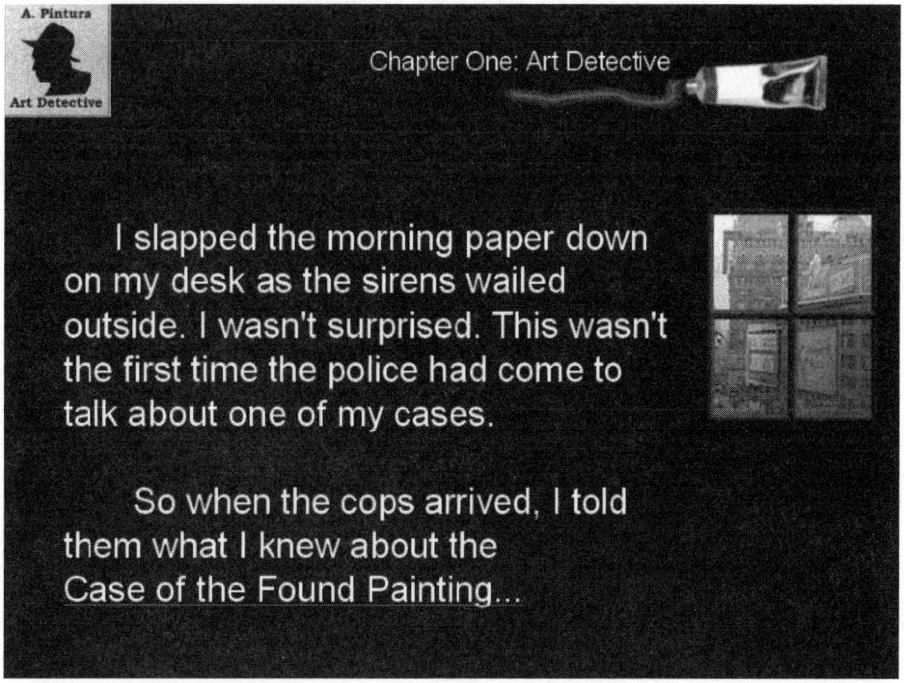

Source: www.eduweb.com/pintura/

in "HungerBanquet" (Figure 2.15). Kevin Thorn's award-winning "Mission: Turfgrass" course (Figure 2.16) puts the learner in the role of a soldier, overcoming pernicious weeds while collecting rewards stored in a rucksack. (The Mission: Turfgrass course itself is at http://learnnuggets. com/portfolio/elearn/turfgrass/player.html.) You will see more examples from these stories in the book.

Figure 2.15. Story: "Hunger Banquet"

You are Gloria Narua

You live in the southern African nation of Mozambique, where you grow crops on a small plot of land. Most years you can produce enough maize, eggplant, carrots, and kale to feed your three children.

You'd like to send your oldest son to school but you can't afford it. He is 9 years old and desperate to learn to read and write. Besides, this year, you'll need his help in the field. Your husband died last spring. People say it could have been AIDS but you can't be sure.

As you look toward the harvest you are worried. The rains were not good this year. This could make for a tough year to come...

≫ **Continue**

Manhemê, Mozambique

≫ **Does Gloria have AIDS?**

Source: www.hungerbanquet.org

Figure 2.16. Story: "Mission: Turfgrass"

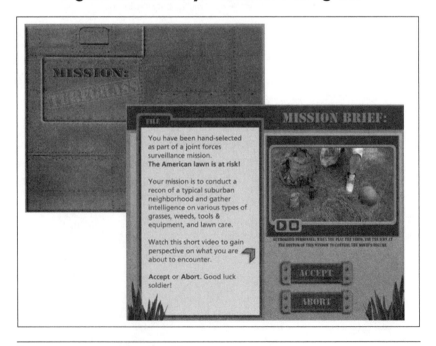

Source: www.nuggethead.net/

From Classroom to Online: Think "Transform," Not "Transfer"

Converting an existing (and presumably successful) classroom course to an online format can be a tricky, time-consuming undertaking. The easy way out—simply moving the content and lecture portions to an electronic means—is what leads to e-"learning" at its worst: slide after slide of bulleted content. Engaging activities and the contributions of individual instructors are lost. Look for ways to capture the richness that a good instructor brings to the classroom, such as responsiveness, a sense of humor, engagement, interesting stories and examples, and immediate feedback. Also, when considering moving a classroom course online, approach it not just as converting one form to another, but as an opportunity to improve the existing product. This is a chance to cull the extraneous, nice-to-know information, to improve what's already there, and to leverage technology for what it can do: for instance, a plain-vanilla paper-and-pencil classroom quiz can be reborn as a dazzling, engaging, seductive online test.

Cut-n-Chunk

This is a good time to reexamine purpose, intent, and objectives. What are the intended outcomes of the program? In order to "work" online, a full-day classroom program must be distilled to its essential elements. Cut out extraneous, "nice to know" information. Is some information population-specific? Is some information tangentially relevant to most but really relevant to none? Every element of the online program should be relevant to most learners. Another issue to consider: How old is the classroom program? How recently was it updated? Is content still current? Are there newer means of delivering the same content, perhaps through electronic aids or other performance support tools?

> An ongoing challenge for e-learning designers is the need to cut, then cut some more. In choosing what to keep and what to edit out, remember the learners first: If they don't use it—lose it!

What's Working? What's Not?

Find out which aspects of the classroom program are most successful—and which fail. Talk with learners and the classroom instructors, and review any evaluation or follow-up data they are able to provide. Are learners leaving the classroom fully prepared to perform successfully back on the job? If not, where are the gaps? Where do instructors feel they need to provide additional explanation? What concepts are difficult to explain? What questions or misunderstandings come up time and again? What opportunities for practice exist in the classroom session? Does the classroom use cases, simulations, and scenarios for practice? What do good individual instructors add to the experience?

Inventory Your Assets

In examining the existing classroom program don't overlook the assets associated with it. Assemble everything—handouts, PowerPoint shows, videos, case studies, evaluation forms—everything associated with the program. There are likely many paper documents—outlines, worksheets, quizzes—that might be repurposed for the online version. Likewise, slide shows, video clips, case studies, and role play information may, too, be useful as part of the e-learning program. Take care not to reinvent the wheel. You may find that much can be adapted for your new purpose.

Converting from Classroom to Online: The Process*

1. Analyze the current state of the classroom program.

2. Update and cut 'n' chunk material.

---

*Model adapted from an online presentation, "Successfully Transitioning Classroom Content to Online Interactivity," by Roni Viles and Katherine Stevens, offered by the e-Learning Guild www.elearningguild.com on July 14, 2006.

3. Identify ways of adding interactivity and capturing richness added by good instructors.

4. Articulate new future state of the (online) program.

5. Storyboard the new online program.

Example: Equal Employment Opportunity Training Program

1. Analyze the current state of the program.

   - Classroom program taught by subject-matter experts (SMEs) in two half-day sessions

   - Extensive lecture-based review of case law

   - Long (two pages) detailed cases focusing on past court issues: learners asked to discuss, but then told "right" answer per the court decision

   - Too much information on laws, little on how to apply

   - "Smile sheet" evaluation only; despite fifteen years of providing program, no research on application back on the job, data as to whether incidents/lawsuits have decreased, etc.

   - SMEs authoritarian, law- and content-focused

   - Learners provided with 110-page spiral-bound manual, no workbook-type activities or exercises, no quick references (FAQs, tabs, color coding, etc.); due to spiral binding no discretion in reorganizing or adding to manual

   - Much content provided elsewhere, as with mandatory unlawful harassment training and hiring programs; many learners already familiar with key ideas/content

   - Heavy emphasis on fact that program is mandated, resulting in many learners as "prisoners"

2. Update and cut-n-chunk.

   - Provide test-out sections so those with prior knowledge can go straight to new learning

   - Seek evaluation beyond smile sheet level to ascertain effectiveness of components

   - Change focus to practical application and desired behavior

   - Move legal details to optional links

   - Eliminate portions that replicate other training

   - Downplay mandate and look for ways to gain interest and voluntary attendance

   - Offer optional supplemental classroom session or provide other mechanism for questions and answers—web meeting, discussion board, etc.

   - Provide questions and situations that provoke reflection on implications, repercussions, etc.

3. Take inventory of assets associated with the classroom program.

   - Manual

   - Video clips (available online for free from a government site)

   - Case studies

4. Identify ways of developing interactivity and capturing contribution of instructors.

   - Use scenarios to teach concepts

   - Provide practical application and exercises

   - Use "What would you do?" scenarios instead of past court decisions

- Provide interactive activities for reinforcement

- Incorporate relevant "war stories" into the online material

5. Articulate the "future state" of the online program.

- Possible treatments: "day in the life" of a manager; judge as narrator/character leading through info; first-person characters explaining their situations; simulation with "What would you do?" scenarios

- Choose treatment and create outline

6. Storyboard the new program.

- The final step in transforming classroom training to PowerPoint-based e-learning: create a storyboard from which to work. This is further discussed in the next section.

Why Storyboard?

The key to making dynamic, effective, interactive PowerPoint-based e-learning is careful planning. Storyboarding and creating mockups of your program will help you organize your thoughts and ensure that your ideas flow logically, without gaps or overkill. It's also a quick, inexpensive way to "test drive" and experiment with your ideas. While you can storyboard in a number of ways, even by sketching on a sheet of paper, PowerPoint is itself a great storyboarding tool. Using the slide sorter view will help you get a "bird's eye view" and see the whole program at once, not just a screen at a time. You might notice that six consecutive screens are text heavy, or there are no opportunities for interaction for a long while. Using the "notes" format (click "view," then "notes page") gives you room below each slide for capturing ideas about navigation, multimedia, and narration, and can provide guidelines for instructional designers or graphic artists with whom you might work. The only drawback: if many people will be reviewing or editing the program you might want to instead choose a tool, such as Word, that allows for tracking changes.

Storyboarding in PowerPoint has another advantage: it can also support your efforts in communicating with other stakeholders connected to your e-learning efforts. Apart from helping you express your vision to graphic designers, the format is usually familiar to clients and helps them to envision the final product better than, say, a long text-only script.

> Remember, the goal of storyboarding is to plan as much as possible before you begin to actually create your online materials. It's much easier to erase or throw away and create new drawings and slides then it is to redesign a completed program!
> **Dede Nelson, Instructional Designer, NC State University**

Types of Storyboards

Let's take a look at different ways of doing storyboards, using a "shark" example, intended for use as an educational program in a museum. Thanks to Ken Loge (www.dreamsteep.com) for the shark materials.

A simple storyboard may just provide a quick overview of your program. Figure 2.17 shows a storyboard drawn by hand; Figure 2.18 illustrates a storyboard created in PowerPoint using the Insert-SmartArt-Hierarchy chart command.

Placing ideas on separate slides, then looking at the program in the slide sorter view, allows you to drag and drop slides to easily rearrange and see how the flow works with different approaches. Figure 2.19 shows the entire program at once in the slide sorter view.

A more detailed storyboard includes notes regarding programming, links, multimedia, etc. Figure 2.20 was created in PowerPoint "normal" view using the text area for speaker notes.

Figure 2.17. Simple Hand-Drawn Storyboard

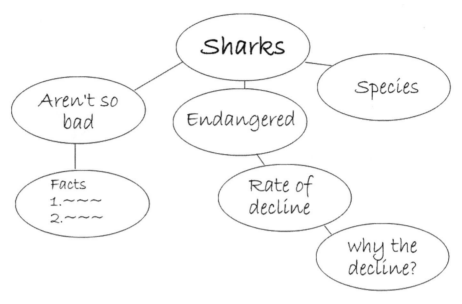

Figure 2.18. Storyboard Created with PowerPoint SmartArt

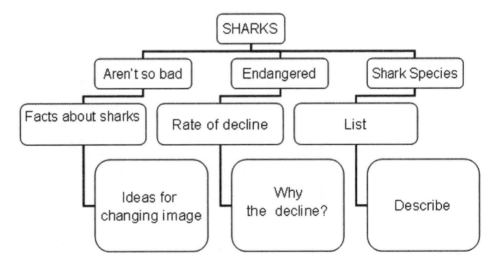

Figure 2.19. PowerPoint Slide Sorter View

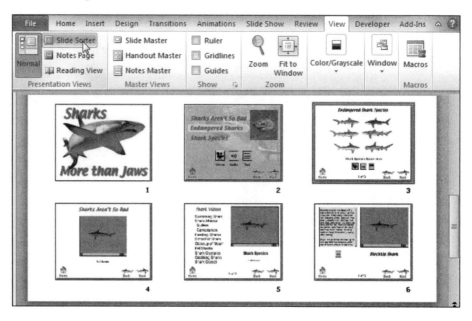

Figure 2.20. Using Speaker Notes Area to Create a Storyboard

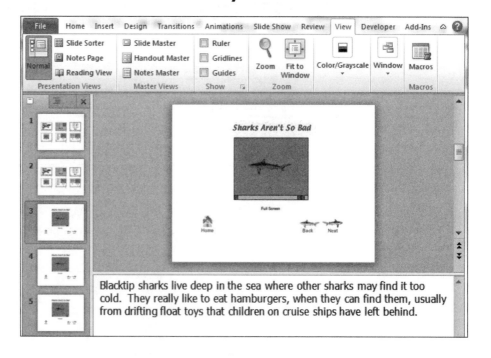

Rather than print out the separate notes pages, I prefer to work from a side-by-side plan; this also provides a convenient script for narrators. Creating a handout will send the PowerPoint show to an editable Word document. To create it choose "File—Save & Send—Create Handouts—Notes Next to Slides," as shown in Figure 2.21.

Learning objectives is where you're going; the storyboard is your road map. There is a big difference between a well-laid-out resource with clear learning objectives and a jumble of badly linked slides.

Dr. Simon James, Lecturer and Multimedia Expert,
University of Tasmania

Figure 2.21. Send PowerPoint File to Word to Create Side-by-Side Storyboard

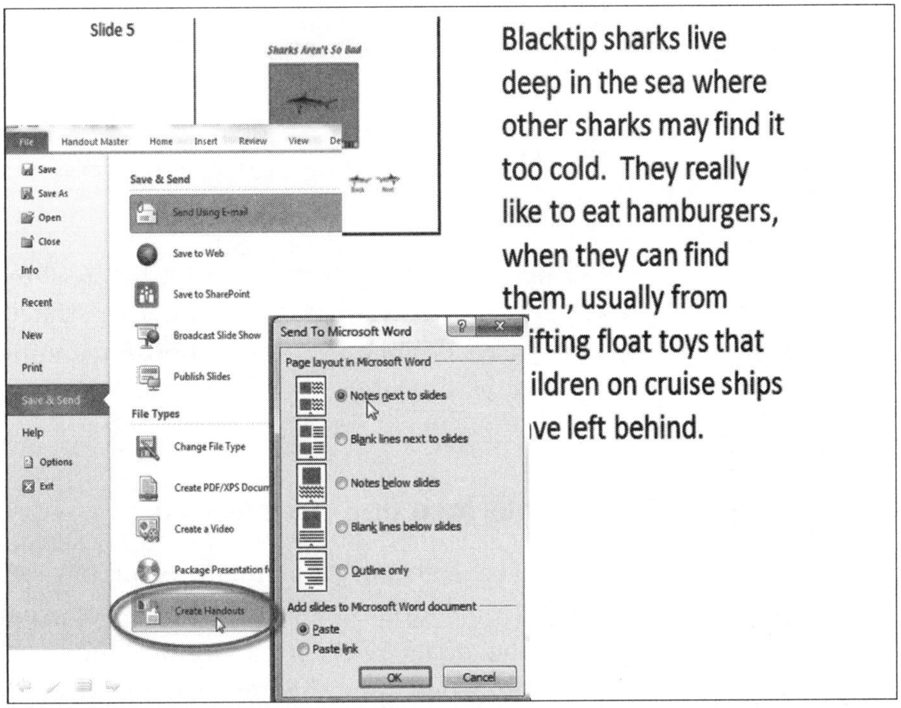

Figure 2.22. Text Storyboard

Slide 1

Title
Shark swims back and
forth. Silly "Jaws"-type
music plays.
Hitting any key or
clicking the mouse
jumps to "Main" screen.
After 1 minute of no
activity, the program
auto-advances to
"Main".

Slide 2

Main
"Home" always goes to
this screen.
Clicking the shark image
goes to the "Title"
screen.
Shark icons set to "next"
and "previous"

Slide 3

Sharks Aren't So Bad
Will need captioning for
those with auditory
impairments

For those doing initial brainstorming, or those working with graphic
designers or other team members, another strategy is to leave the
PowerPoint slides blank pending choosing graphics, inserting media,
etc., as shown in Figure 2.22.

Next Stop: The Program Interface and Architecture

An effective e-learning program grows out of careful identification of
learners, articulation of objectives, and an approach that supports the
instructional goals. While it's tempting, when working with PowerPoint,
to just open a new slide show and start adding content, the time spent

in specifying outcomes and storyboarding will pay off in ease of development and reduction of rework and piloting time. If you are working to transform an existing classroom program to an online format, this phase of development is a good time to examine what's working—or not—with the classroom sessions and ensure that the new program provides opportunities for learning, rather than just parroting the content of the classroom program. Being mindful of the principles of good instruction, especially the new considerations of multimedia that e-learning demands, will help to ensure the success of your program.

Now that you have some understanding of the basics of instructional design for e-learning purposes, we'll move on into development issues. The next chapter covers the learner's relationship with your program: look, feel, navigation, and the graphic interface.

Interface and Content

Graphic User Interface and Course Architecture

n developing your e-learning program, it is vital that you create a user-friendly interface with clear information on how to navigate the course. Additionally, your program will need a unified look and feel in terms of colors and any branding elements that your organization requires. In designing an interface you'll also need to consider the overall structure of your course. Is this a single, short stand-alone topic, or will instruction be provided in several modules? Will learners need to access material in a particular sequence, or can they skip around the subtopics within a program. Use your storyboard as a tool for identifying manageable chunks, modules, and basic ideas about organizing the final program.

This chapter covers concepts related to the GUI, navigation, course architecture, and considerations of learner control. There is also information on setting up overall course architecture as well as an introduction to the use of action buttons and hyperlinking.

The website for this book includes tutorials for several tasks covered in this chapter, including working with slide masters, inserting action settings, and using navigation tools.

Graphic User Interface

A critical factor in the success of an e-learning program is the learner's view of it. Known as the "graphical user interface" (known as the GUI, or "gooey," and now sometimes shortened to just UI), it establishes the user's relationship with the program, or the dialogue between the learner and the training. Think of the GUI as, essentially, the e-learning program's dashboard, containing links, icons, buttons, and other navigational tools, and any of the branding elements associated with the program. As with most things related to e-learning, less is more: your goal should be to create an attractive, clean interface that gives the learner clear direction about what to do next (see Figure 3.1). The carefully designed GUI supports the learner; the poor one can cause the learner to give up in frustration.

Figure 3.1. Clean, Clear Interface

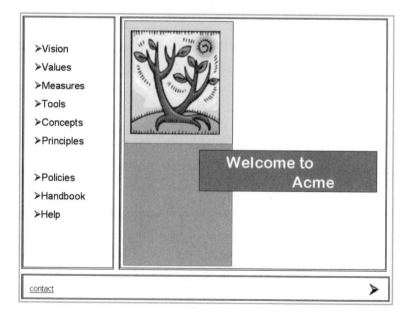

GUI Basics

In designing the GUI, keep in mind that online learners need to always know four things:

1. What to do next

2. How to get home

3. What's going on

4. How to get out

Some tips for a good interface:

- Be consistent and clear. Don't use an arrow on one screen and a "next" link on another.

- At a minimum, the program should include navigational information indicating next screen, previous screen, home screen, and links to help and/or contact information. Learners need to know how to exit, although, depending on how you choose to distribute the course (see Chapter 10) you may just instruct them to close the browser. PowerPoint has transparent navigation already built in; that is, any mouse click will take the learner to the next screen. (If you don't want learners just clicking along, you can disable this feature by clicking "slide show-slide transition" and unchecking the option to "advance on mouse click" and choosing "apply to all slides.")

- Use clear, consistent icons. Don't assume that learners will understand that a white flag icon means "help." Labeling the icons on the first screen never hurts.

- Most programs contain a menu to an outline of different topics, segments, or modules (an example is shown in Figure 3.1). Short, single-topic programs may be the exception. Some programs also have an opening table of contents screen.

- You may also link to other tools, a glossary, contact information, or set an email link for submitting questions or asking for help

- If you are using audio or video, include information for learners so they will know how to adjust the volume on their computers.

- Consider including a screen counter or progress bar to indicate to learners how much of the program has been completed/how much is left.

- Tell learners what's happening. Often video clips take a moment to load, or there may be a delay as documents open. Advise learners of this so they don't assume something's wrong. Include information such as, "Click here to open a Word document . . ." or "This link will take you to an online quiz." Figure 3.2 shows an example.

Figure 3.2. Slide Counter and "What's Happening"

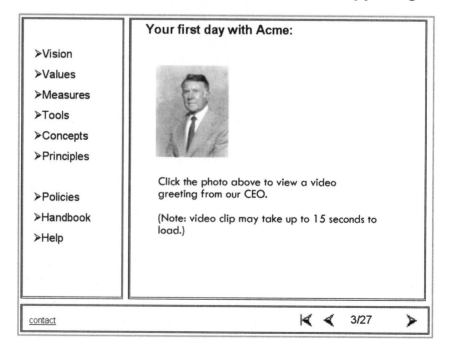

The overall structure of your course may determine how you design the GUI. The "Acme" example in Figure 3.2 works much like a web page, allowing learners to click on links to access information on particular topics. The GUI in Figure 3.3, from a simulation requiring learners to move in a more linear manner, offers a "forward" button with directions explicitly stated in the text (circled here for readers). The "x" at the top right corner allows learners to exit the program, while the small upward arrow returns learners to the home screen.

Other GUIs might be developed around a theme or the chosen treatment. The "A. Pintura: Art Detective" program, introduced earlier in the book and shown again in Figure 3.4, is developed as a noir-type mystery. The overall look is a black screen, with plain white text, and simple underlined navigation links. Most screens ask the learners to make a choice about where to go next, rather than just prompting them to move to the following slide.

Figure 3.3. Simple GUI

Source: Royal Veterinary College

Figure 3.4. GUI from "A. Pintura: Art Detective"

Source: www.eduweb.com

Colors

When thinking about the overall look of your program, remember that color has meaning:

- RED: warning, danger, heat, stop

- GREEN: go, money

- BLUE: calm

Color may also have cultural implications. In the United States, for example, white indicates purity. In Asian cultures it is the color of death.

Learner Control: Some Decisions

As the trainer/designer you will need to make some decisions about the degree of control your learners will have. e-Learning programs often include a navigation button that indicates "last" screen. Providing such an option means that a learner could, if he or she wanted, just skip to the end of the e-learning program from any other screen. It's up to you whether you want to give learners that much discretion. Likewise, if your program is modular or arranged by topics, will you allow the learner to visit sections as she likes, or will you force some sort of sequence? Realize, too, that learners likely have experience surfing the web and are used to making choices about where to go next and what content they wish to view.

On a philosophical note: it is the nature of e-learning to require discretion and self-direction on the part of learners, and at some point we must learn to trust them. Consider the learner in a "live" class who leaves the room for three minutes to take a phone call. Do we say that person is not "complete"? Why is it that skipping a screen of an e-learning program is considered so much more serious? Similarly, unless the content of the e-learning program is teaching a step-by-step procedure, why shouldn't the learner be allowed to choose the order in which to view topics? While you don't want learners getting "lost" in your program, engagement and persistence are supported by learners feeling a sense of control.

Navigation Tools and Action Buttons

For basic navigation, PowerPoint will let the learner advance to the next slide just by clicking the space bar or "Enter" key, but you will need to be sure to communicate this to the learner. An e-learning program more often will have buttons, arrows, or other symbols indicating "next" to the learner. An easy solution here is inserting PowerPoint's customizable action buttons (shown in Figure 3.5).

Figure 3.5. Action Buttons Included with PowerPoint

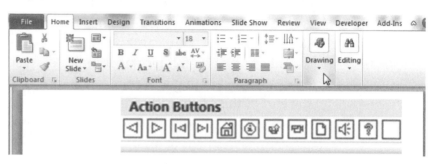

 See the website for tutorials on working with action settings and navigation.

These buttons are preprogrammed for actions such as "next slide" and "first slide," but can easily be reset to link to any other slide, file, or even external site, and can provide the learner with visual cues for moving through the program. The action buttons can be found in the "shapes" tools found in the "drawing" area from the home tab (see Figure 3.5). (*Note:* Throughout the rest of the book, instructions for accessing a particular command or tool will be noted as "shapes—action buttons.") After choosing a button, browse for the destination link (Figure 3.6).

PowerPoint also allows for much more sophisticated navigation through the use of hyperlinks. The designer can create hyperlinks from text boxes, graphics, and other elements placed on a slide. These will take the learner from this selected "hotspot" or "hot object" (or whole slide) to another slide within the same show, another PowerPoint show, a website, or a document such as a Word or PDF file. A hyperlink to an email address will, when clicked, open an already-addressed email window on the learner's computer screen.

Hyperlinks within a program can be inserted in one of two ways: by selecting an object and giving it an action setting, as shown with the button in Figure 3.7, or by right-clicking on the object, choosing "hyperlink"

Figure 3.6. Setting Action Buttons

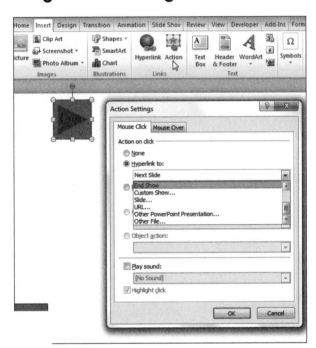

Figure 3.7. PowerPoint's Action Buttons Can Be Customized

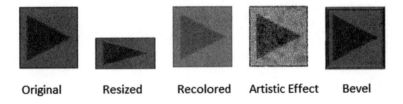

Original   Resized   Recolored   Artistic Effect   Bevel and selecting the link's destination. Figure 3.8 shows the example of a program's outline page. When viewed in slide show mode clicking on the "what" box will take the learner directly to the "what" slide. See Figure 3.9 to see how this interaction was created. (Note, as shown in Figure 3.9, the options for hyperlinking to an existing file or web page, to another slide within the current PowerPoint show, or to an email address.)

Figure 3.8. Choose "Insert-Hyperlink" and Browse for Destination Slide

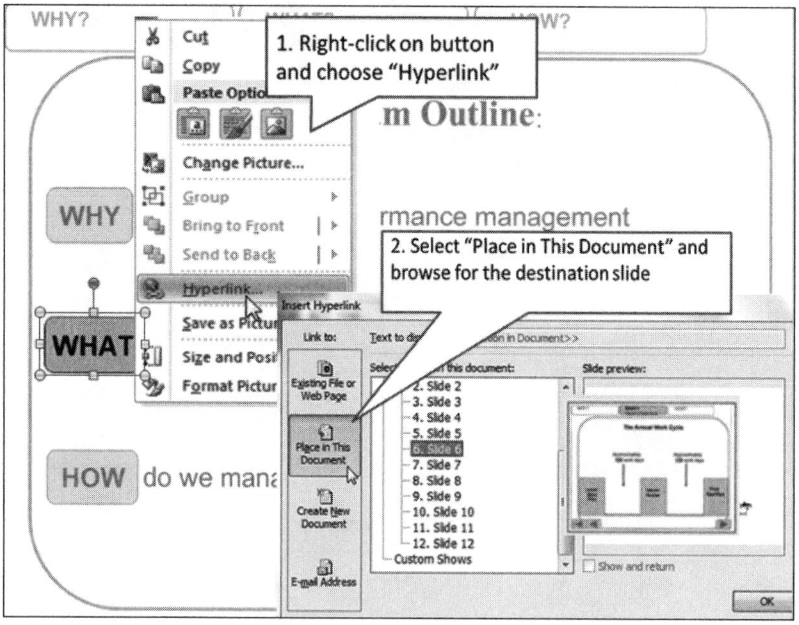

You may also find that the action buttons or shapes included with PowerPoint do not meet your design needs. Navigation symbols can be created from other objects, arrows, words, or simple linked text. Programming is done by highlighting the item and clicking "insert-hyperlink," as shown in Figure 3.9. Figure 3.10 shows an array of choices for navigational tools found during a simple search of www .google.com for "free navigation buttons and icons"; the shark icons are from the storyboarding examples in Chapter 2.

Interface design has nothing to do with instructional design but has everything to do with effective e-learning. Proper placement of buttons, navigational aids, and screen tools can make or break your e-learning project, no matter how effective the instructional design.

Thomas Toth, *Technology for Trainers.*

Figure 3.9. Varied Options for Navigation Tools

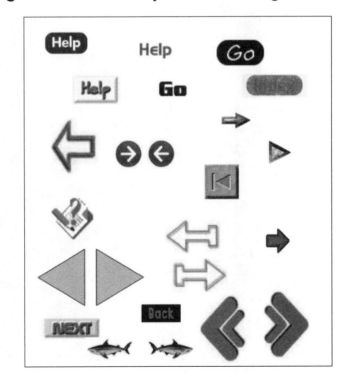

Eye Movement and Placement of Items

In designing the GUI for your program it's important that you understand the basics of eye movement. Think about reading: when you read
a page your eyes move across the top line from left to right, then drop
down to the second line at the far left, and then continue left to right
again. This "Z" movement is the most natural and intuitive for learners.
A good GUI makes use of this Z movement to support clarity, ease of
use, and emphasis. Figure 3.10 shows a GUI created to accommodate
the eye's natural Z movement. Important content is given "center
stage", while supporting information, like links and navigation icons,

Figure 3.10. Good GUI Recognizes "Z" Eye Movement

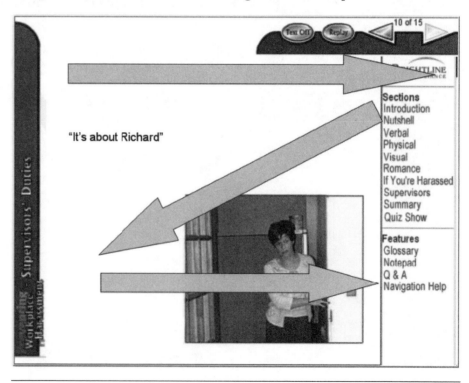

Source: www.brightlinecompliance.com

are placed in positions of less emphasis. Information across the top of the screen communicates the learner's location in terms of subject, topic, segment, or chapter. Also note how the placement of the "next" arrow pointer button naturally leads the eye off the screen and toward the next one.

You are probably already aware of some unspoken standards of designing for the web, although you may not have given it much thought. Most designers know to develop with the Z in mind, and users are, generally, accustomed to looking to the left side of the screen for links.

Working with Z eye movement in mind supports what is known in the web world as maximizing your screen "real estate." Figure 3.11 illustrates the real estate concept. How long does it take to even notice the line that says "nearly invisible"?

Figure 3.11. Value of Screen "Real Estate"

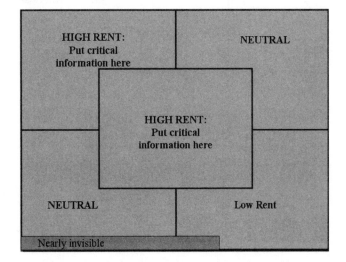

Lesson Learned

In maximizing your screen real estate, watch out for how much space logos and other branding elements consume. Consider placing logos and similar items only on the first and last slides rather than on all slides.

Figures 3.12 through 3.15 show additional problems with GUIs.

Figure 3.12. Common Problems with GUIs

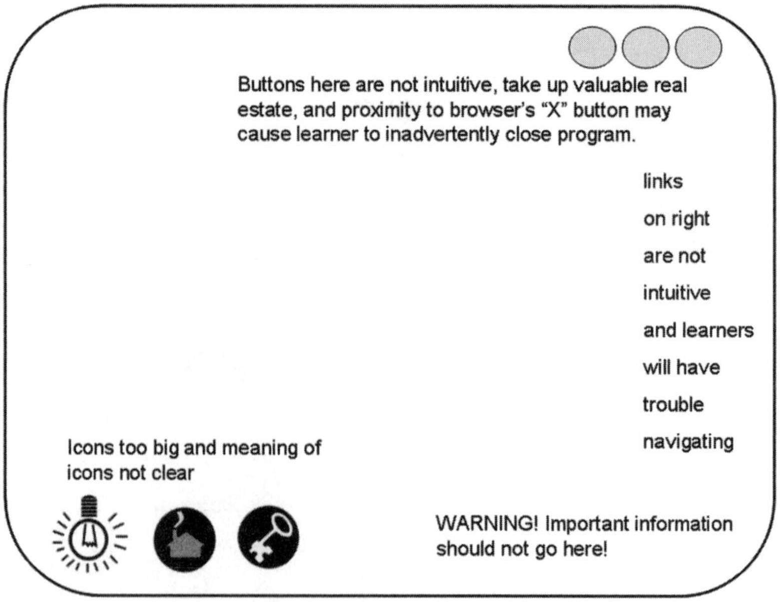

Buttons here are not intuitive, take up valuable real estate, and proximity to browser's "X" button may cause learner to inadvertently close program.

links

on right

are not

intuitive

and learners

will have

trouble

Icons too big and meaning of   navigating
icons not clear

WARNING! Important information
should not go here!

Figure 3.13. Background Makes Text Hard to Read

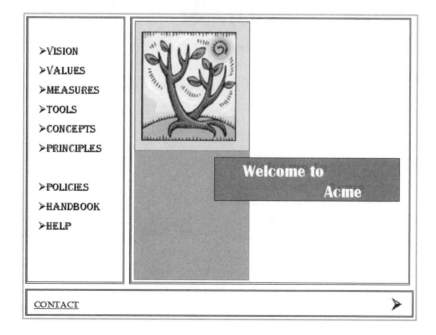

Figure 3.14. Fonts Are Hard to Read

Figure 3.15. Font Color Does Not Sharply Contrast

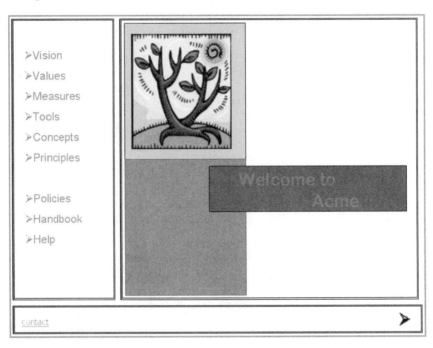

Lesson Learned

As you develop your e-learning program, see how it displays on
other computer screens. Different monitors display colors differently; what looks like good contrast on your screen may look like
faded text on another.

Building the GUI

Again, think of the GUI as a sort of template defining the look, feel, and
navigation basics for your e-learning program. This is a matter of

creating slide masters by adding elements that will make up your new interface.

Create a Slide Master

Using a slide master will make your job much easier. Slide masters make for consistent, professional appearance: insert objects that will appear on each slide, including any branding elements, navigation items, etc. The slide master functions, essentially, as a template for the screens in your e-learning program. Open the slide master by clicking "view—master—slide master," as shown in Figure 3.16. Note that the master is set up for text-based basic presentation slides; you can highlight and delete slide areas you don't need (like the title running across the near center of the screen), although they will not, unless you add to them, appear on the final slides. Figures 3.16 through 3.19 show steps in creating a slide master for use in an e-learning program.

Also see the website for a tutorial on working with slide masters.

Figure 3.16. Access the Slide Master View

Figure 3.17. Blank Slide Master

Figure 3.18. Add Navigation Elements, in This Case, Buttons

Figure 3.19. Completed Program

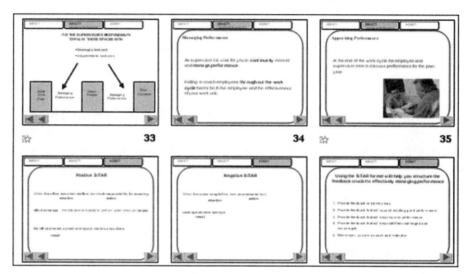

If for some reason you want a slide within the same program to differ from others—for instance, if you need a title or "home" slide or module introduction slides different from the rest of the program—you can achieve this by creating multiple slide masters. Click "view—slide master." When the master toolbar appears click "insert new."

Lesson Learned

When developing a long program or one with several modules, create separate PowerPoint shows rather than one long show. This will make editing, managing, and updating materials much less cumbersome and will help keep file sizes to reasonable levels.

Examples: Creating the GUI

Figures 3.20 through 3.24 show different styles of GUIs and how they were created.

Figure 3.20. Slide Master for Program Uses Shapes

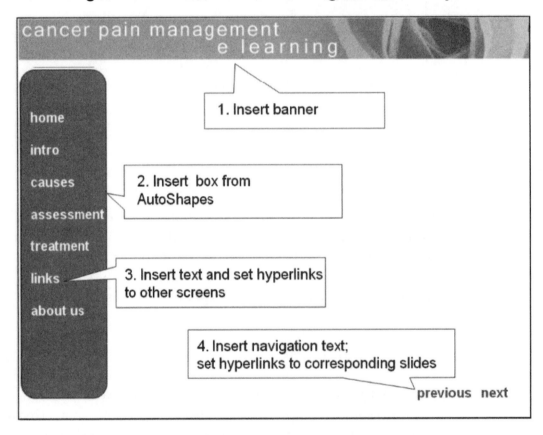

Figure 3.21. Each Screen Will Look like This

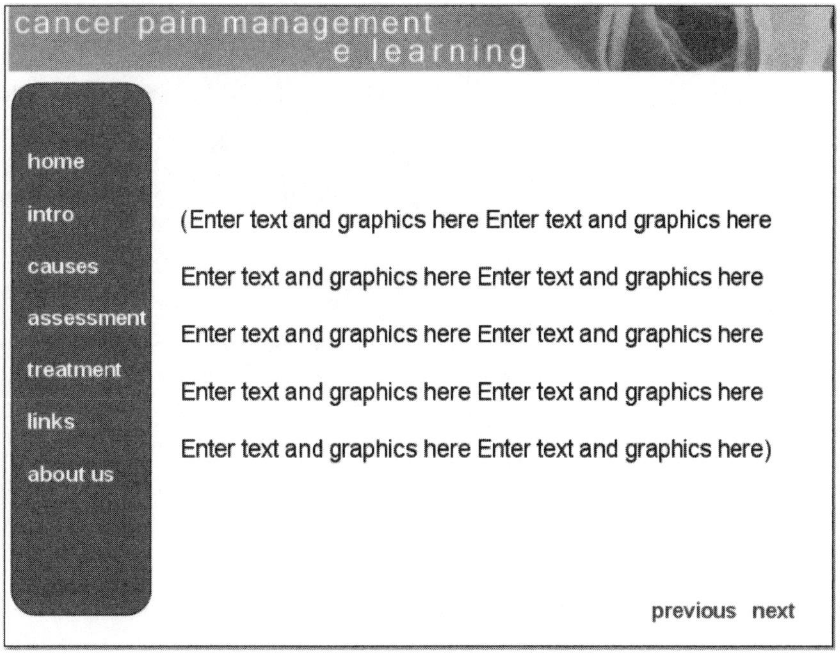

cancer pain management
e learning

home

intro

causes

assessment

treatment

links

about us

(Enter text and graphics here Enter text and graphics here

Enter text and graphics here Enter text and graphics here

Enter text and graphics here Enter text and graphics here

Enter text and graphics here Enter text and graphics here

Enter text and graphics here Enter text and graphics here)

previous next

Note: The "Cancer Pain Management" interface is adapted from an existing online program and is used here with the generous permission of Dr. Mahibur Rahman, Director, Emedica. The program can be accessed in full, for free, at www.emedica.co.uk. Click the "e-learning" link.

Figures 3.22 and 3.23 show a main screen with tabbed navigation; subsequent screens have links to topics. Figure 3.24 shows how tabs were created with Shapes.

 The website includes a narrated explanation of how this GUI was created.

Figure 3.22. GUI with Tabbed Navigation

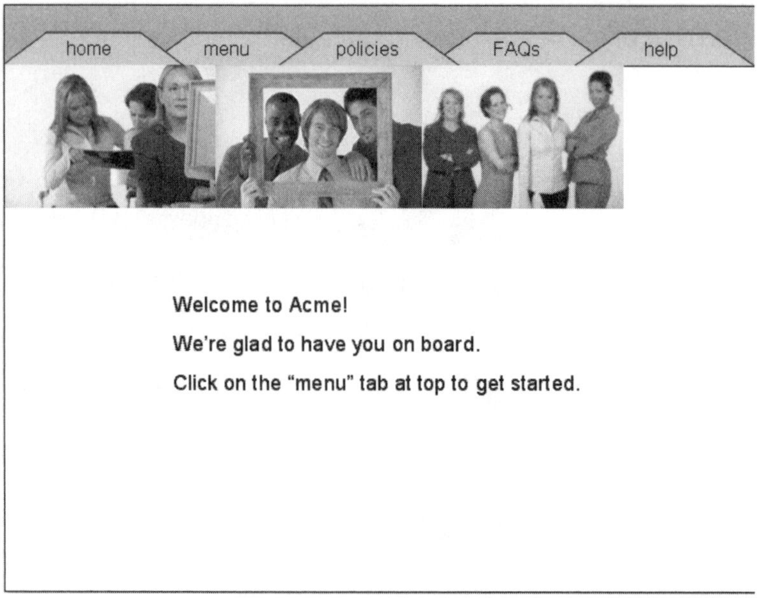

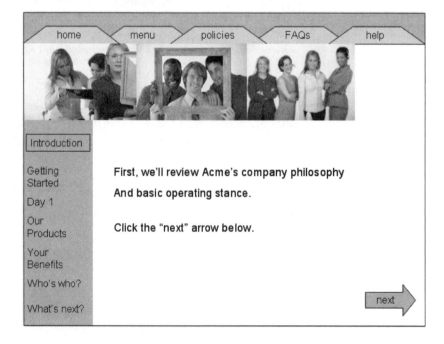

Figure 3.23. Subsequent Slides Contain Links to Topics

Figure 3.24. Steps in Creating Screen Including Tabs for Navigation

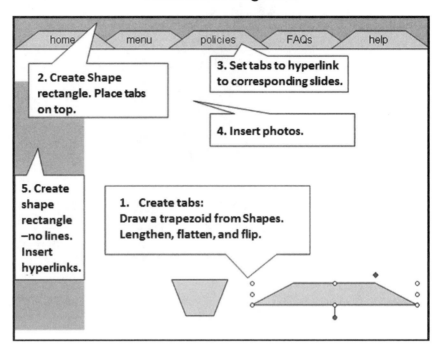

Figure 3.24 shows how to create this screen.

In developing the GUI it's okay to be creative provided that learners have clear guidance. Figure 3.25 shows navigation based on icons: images link to the corresponding topics.

Figure 3.25. Icon-Based Navigation

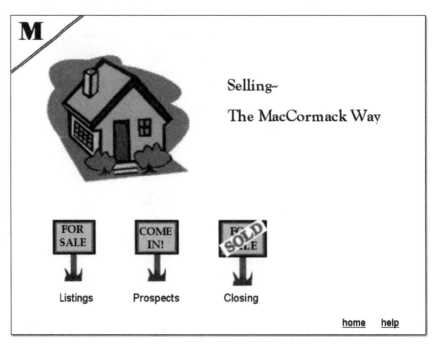

The examples in Figures 3.26 and 3.27 are also icon-based but use none of the traditional navigational markers (arrows, "next," even words indicating topics) but it's easy enough to tell that the program is linear and to determine the order in which screens should be viewed.

Figure 3.26. Icon-Based Navigation Without Markers

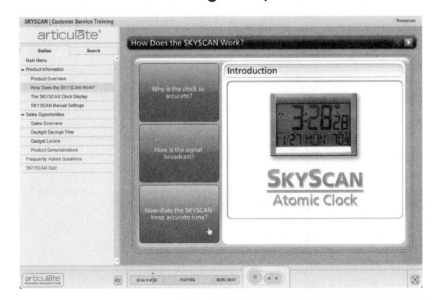

Adapted from program by Laura Bergell www.maniactive.com

Figure 3.27. Button-Based Navigation (Shown in Articulate Player)

Used with permission of Tom Kuhlmann

Lesson Learned

When testing your e-learning program, actually sit and watch learners going through it. What seems intuitive or clear to you may not be clear to them—and watching them interact with the material will give you ideas about how to fix it. This will also give you a sense of how much time different screens, quizzes, or interactions may take to complete.

Architecture

Although there are no hard and fast rules, most e-learning courses will contain some similar elements. These usually include:

- A title and/or "welcome" slide.

- An advance organizer: as noted in Richard Mayer's "SOI" model discussed in Chapter 3, it's important to provide learners with a course outline, statement of objectives, or explanation of course structure. Figure 3.28 shows an example.

Figure 3.28. Advance Organizer

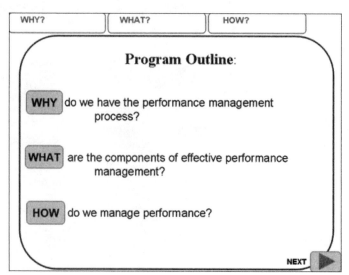

Figure 3.29. Explanation of Navigation

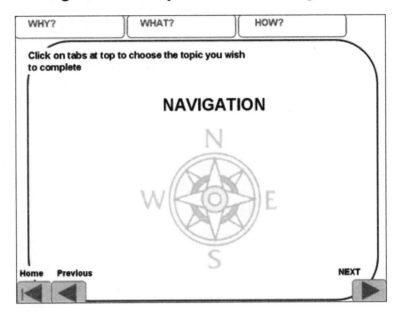

- An explanation of how to use the course, as shown in Figure 3.29. The words "home," "previous," and "next" do not appear on subsequent screens. If you are using media, you may need to also add information about controlling the volume of audio or video clips.

- A glossary of terms and acronyms.

- A site map is especially important with modular programs created with PowerPoint: as PowerPoint does not support bookmarking, learners cannot leave a program and subsequently return to the same screen. A site map allows them to get back to the general area where they left off. The site map also lets learners search a program and return to parts they wish to review. Figure 3.30 shows an example of a site map.

Figure 3.30. Example of a Site Map

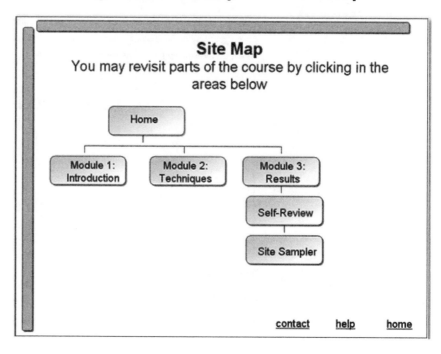

Other architectural elements—such as the sequence of slides, the placement of modules, and the layout of branching interactions, can be pulled from your program storyboard.

Excuse My Rant

While I receive many requests for one, I will not provide, do not advocate, and do not use a single course "template," and I am wary of vendors offering such things. While all courses need some basic elements—such as a home page—the concept of a single multi-slide template appropriate to all e-learning programs supports the erroneous notion that e-learning can be created by simply dumping content onto slides. And it creates the temptation to do just that. Such templates might be fine for informational presentations, but are anathema to good training. Examples of engaging e-learning programs like the "A. Pintura: Art Detective" mystery and the "Gamekeeper's Conundrum" simulation came from solid, creative design and would never have been developed had the designers started by trying to shovel content into predetermined screens or worked from some preconceived notion of how courses should look. Be brave! Be creative!

Next Stop: Designing for Impact

Although it may seem tedious, creating a good GUI and a clear organizational structure will save work (and re-work) in the long run. (As designer J.D. Dillon says, "Bad interface design can ruin great content.") Now the real fun starts: adding the content to your e-learning program. Chapter 4 offers guidelines for conveying your message and avoiding blunders.

Designing for Impact

Use Graphics with Soul

In choosing images that will support your instructional message, give real thought to what will help you convey intent and support your learners. There are a number of excellent, extensive clipart, photo, and sound galleries, among them the Microsoft office gallery (http://office.microsoft.com/en-us/clipart/default.aspxs), iStockphoto (www.istockphoto.com), and Clipart.com (www.clipart.com); the trick, however, is not in choosing an image but in choosing the right one. Jamie McKenzie, editor of *From Now On: The Educational Technology Journal*, rails against what he calls "mulitmediocracy" and encourages us to look beyond first glances at clipart galleries to find graphics with soul. The example on the next page illustrates the problem of choosing the right graphic for an online tutorial on email etiquette, designed primarily to convey the fact that email is not private. A quick search of clipart galleries provides many images, such as those shown in Figure 4.1, but most are too cutesy, too busy, or just indecipherable for the purpose of the tutorial:

Figure 4.1. Images from Clipart Gallery Search for "Email"

Compare this to Figure 4.2 below, which puts a human (implicitly, the learner) into the message. Additionally, the grayscale effect suggests the seriousness of the topic.

What Conveys the Message?

As with the topic above, some programs implicitly demand graphics that are serious and authoritative. This is especially important with most medical, legal, and compliance-related programs. Looking at Figure 4.3, with photos taken from the same clip and photo art gallery, which doctor would you want to perform your open heart surgery?

Figure 4.2. Graphic with Soul for the Email Etiquette Program

Thanks to www.indezine.com for free background template

Figure 4.3. Choose Your Heart Surgeon

As we discussed in Chapter 2, it is crucial that you be clear, before you begin developing your e-learning program, about what you are trying to accomplish. The right graphic can set the tone, establish a mood, and support the instructional message. Look at the examples that follow.

Example 1: Civil Rights Timeline

The first image of this timeline, shown in Figure 4.4, presents data about civil rights legislation. Figure 4.5 shows how the addition of the right photograph supports the data in conveying a sense of history and the struggles behind those rights.

Figure 4.4. Civil Rights Timeline

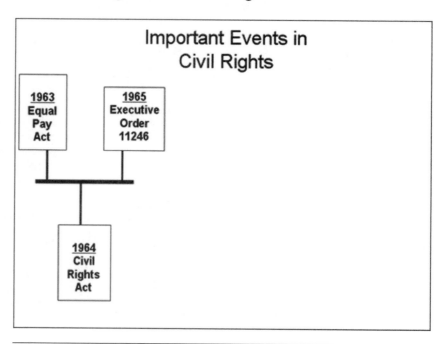

Courtesy of Paige Dosser

Figure 4.5. Addition of Watts Riot Photo

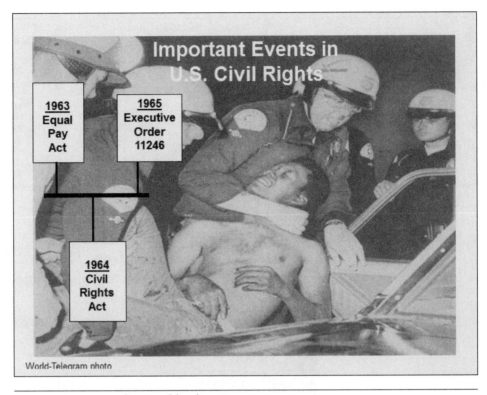

Source: Watts Riot photo: public domain

Example 2: Vietnam Vets

In Example 2, the designer wanted to create an awareness of the need—and support for—funding for treatment for aging veterans. The typical approach, shown in Figure 4.6, would likely include a title slide, bar chart showing data about the problem, then a bulleted list of possible solutions. Figure 4.7 shows the same topic, revised to begin with just the image of the Vietnam Memorial. The updated program opens with a long silence, then a narrator saying, "Our vets need us now. . . ."

Figure 4.6. Typical Approach to Request for Support

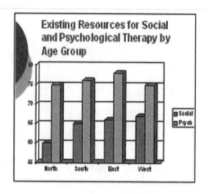

Figure 4.7. Information from Figure 4.6 Provided as Voiceover to This Image

Thanks to Seth Godin (www.sethgodin.com) for the "Vietnam vet" example

"Let Me Show You What I Mean"

The just-right image conveys the message, "Let me show you what I mean." What is the essence of what you are trying to say? Try to distill your message and intent. A good exercise is to take any text-based slide and try to re-create it with images. The next few figures illustrate the difference this can make with a program on "cubicle etiquette." The first slide, Figure 4.8, shows a text-only version of one screen. Figure 4.9 shows the same message distilled into images drawn from a clip art gallery. Even before the addition of voiceover explanation, the second slide is much more effective, engaging, and memorable.

Figure 4.8. Text-Only Slide

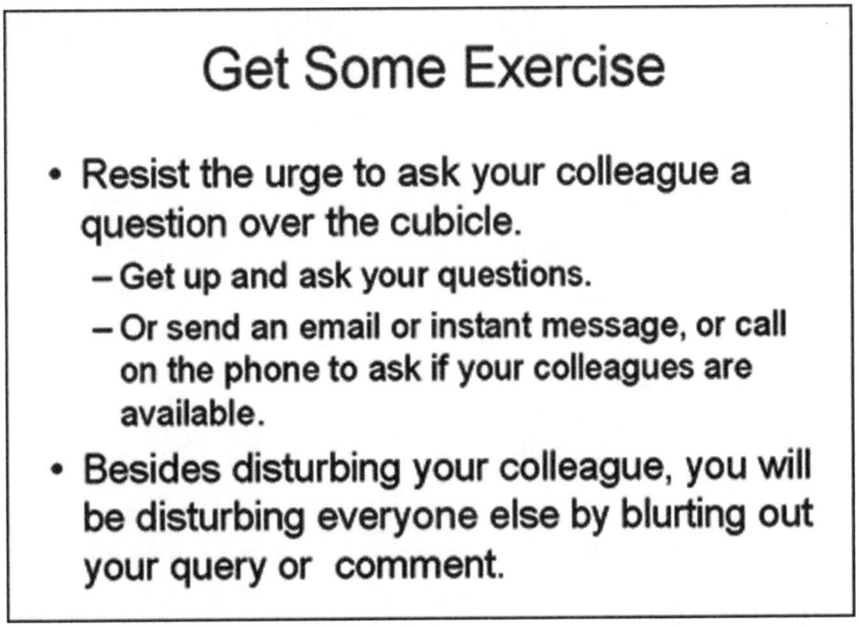

Get Some Exercise

- **Resist the urge to ask your colleague a question over the cubicle.**
  - Get up and ask your questions.
  - Or send an email or instant message, or call on the phone to ask if your colleagues are available.
- **Besides disturbing your colleague, you will be disturbing everyone else by blurting out your query or comment.**

Source: "Cubicle Etiquette" by Gary Michael Smith, *Intercom* magazine, November 2000

Figure 4.9. Same Slide Re-Created with Graphics Instead of Text

Source: "Cubicle Etiquette." Thanks to Patricia Delaney

The example in Figures 4.10 through 4.12, screens from an online program teaching learners to read diagrams of electrical circuits, shows how simple graphics with minimal clutter can make a complex idea understandable. In this case, the designer moved from images of a completed circuit, to a legend explaining each image, then finally a "textbook" diagram of the circuit.

In some cases it may be that a diagram, rather than an image, is worth a thousand words. Use of the right diagram—such as a flowchart or a pyramid showing hierarchical relationships—proves invaluable in clarifying information and supports per Mayer's (Chapter 2) guidelines on providing instruction in ways that will help the learner organize it. Diagrams can easily be created with PowerPoint's SmartArt, shown in Figure 4.13.

Figure 4.10. Slide 1 Shows the Completed Circuit

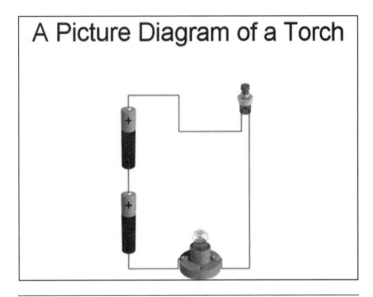

Electric circuit program copyright Simon Drane; electric circuit
component images are from www.crocodile-clips.com

Figure 4.11. Slide 2 Explains the Symbols

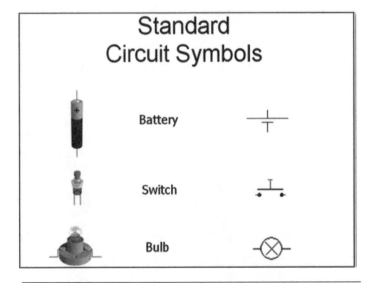

Electric circuit program copyright Simon Drane; electric circuit
component images are from www.crocodile-clips.com

Figure 4.12. Slide 3 Provides a Schematic of the Circuit

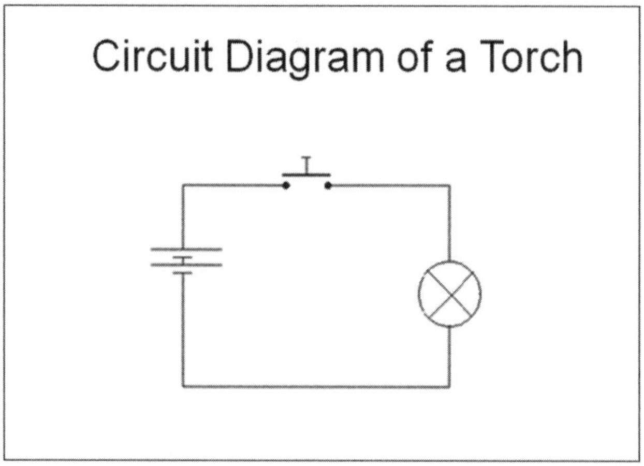

Circuit Diagram of a Torch

Electric circuit program copyright Simon Drane; electric circuit component images are from www.crocodile-clips.com

Figure 4.13. Diagrams in PowerPoint's SmartArt Gallery

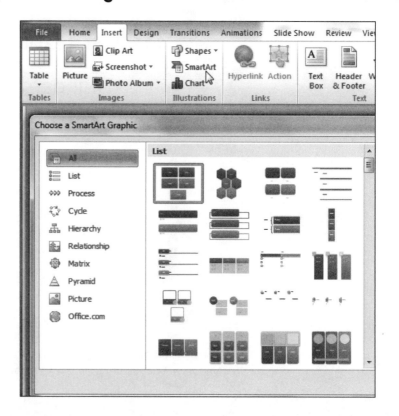

Is There a Visual Here?

Sometimes we get so caught up in explaining a concept that we forget to take a step back and look for a visual of the idea. Figure 4.14 shows a screen with details about the content required for a disciplinary warning letter. Figure 4.15 shows the same information, but in a realistic—and more memorable—context.

Figure 4.14. Before: Text List of Required Items

Written Warning

Definition:
    A detailed disciplinary notice for conduct or performance

A Written Warning Must:
    State that it is a warning
    State the reason for the warning
    Detail the improvements required
    Indicate length of time allowed for improvement
    State the consequences if improvements are
       not made
    Outline the appeal process

Figure 4.15. After: Sample Letter Shows Items in Realistic Context

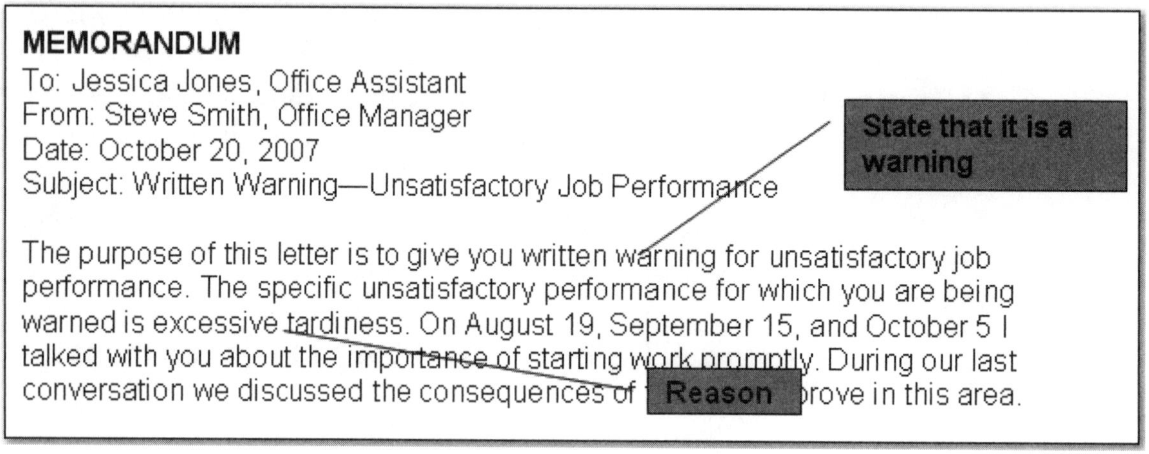

MEMORANDUM
To: Jessica Jones, Office Assistant
From: Steve Smith, Office Manager
Date: October 20, 2007
Subject: Written Warning—Unsatisfactory Job Performance

State that it is a warning

The purpose of this letter is to give you written warning for unsatisfactory job performance. The specific unsatisfactory performance for which you are being warned is excessive tardiness. On August 19, September 15, and October 5 I talked with you about the importance of starting work promptly. During our last conversation we discussed the consequences of [Reason] prove in this area.

Blunders

It is easy to be seduced by galleries of entertaining images and interesting fonts. Some common mistakes are illustrated below.

Dreadful Design

The slide shown in Figure 4.16 shows many of the most typical design flaws, from too much content to illegible text to space-hogging template elements.

Decoration

Figure 4.17 makes use of a cute graphic that has nothing to do with the training or the message on the screen. Learners will wonder, "What does loyalty have to do with a bee lifting weights?"

Figure 4.16. Example of Design Mistakes

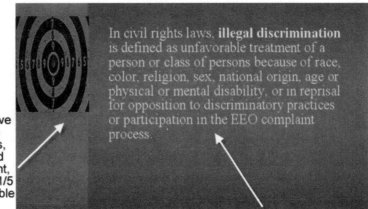

Decorative template elements, unrelated to content, take up 1/5 of available space

Font too small to be legible, far too much text, white text hard to read on 'shimmery' background. Slide is informational, not instructional.

Figure 4.17. Decorative Graphic

Noise

"Noise" refers not only to sound but to clutter and extraneous information on a screen. If I want, for instance, to discuss the details of just one slide, I need to show only that. Figure 4.18 shows the slide, but includes a view of my whole desktop screen, opened to a full view of the PowerPoint program, while Figure 4.19 shows just the slide with no other information around it.

Figure 4.20 shows problems with noise on a single slide. The preset template is cluttered with items unrelated to the content, including a sidebar, decorative dotted line, and a heavy line below the heading. The cute clipart image only tangentially relates to the concept. The callout star is distracting and, due to brightness, appears to be the most important element on the screen. The shadowed text and crowded font make the letters run together. Finally, all the lines of text of similar size compete with each other: What is this slide about?

**Figure 4.18. Slide Includes Too Much
Extraneous Information**

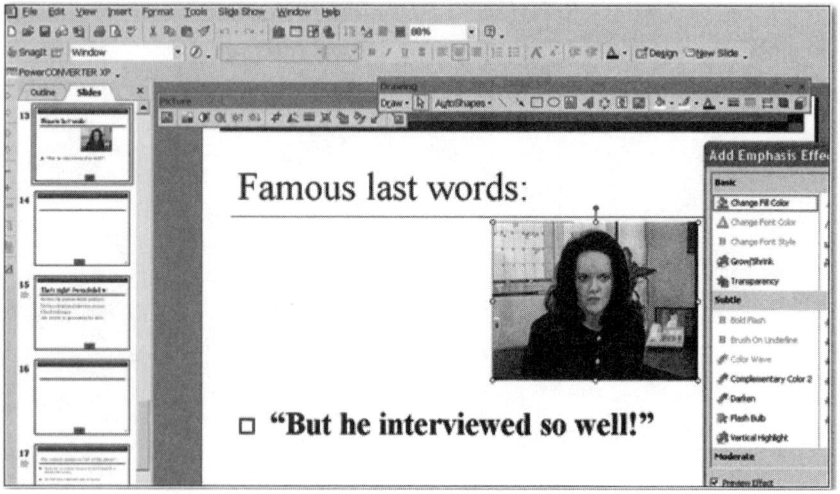

Figure 4.19. Extraneous Information Removed

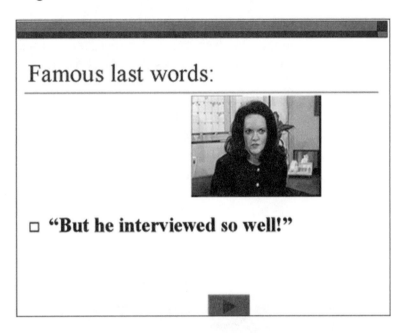

Figure 4.20. This Screen Is Too "Noisy" to Be Effective

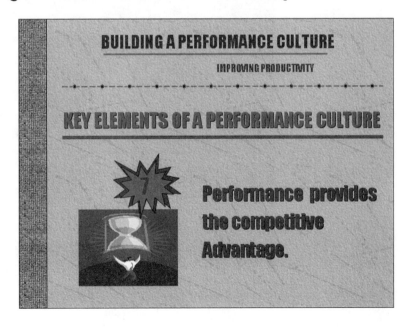

Demeaning

Sometimes the temptation to use a cute piece of art overrides good judgment. The designers of Figures 4.21 and 4.22 probably meant well, but ended up with images that are insulting to learners.

Finally, try to move beyond working toward one graphic at a time or matching a graphic to template elements, and consider the overall look of your course. PowerPoint doesn't have to look "PowerPoint-y." Figure 4.23 is a nice example from Trina Rimmer showing the before-and-after design work on a project.

Figure 4.21. Insulting Approach

Figure 4.22. Insulting Approach

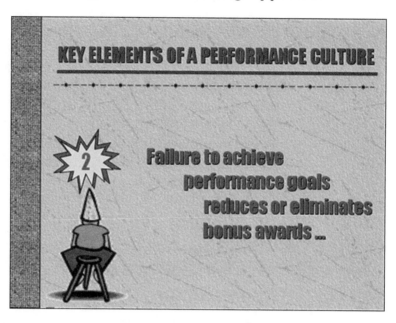

Figure 4.23. Before-and-After Overall Design Using PowerPoint

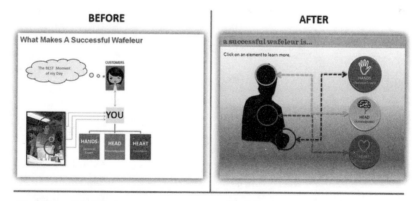

The Before: This click n' read training presentation for a start-up gourmet food company suffered from clashing clipart and didn't reflect the company's fun, quirky brand.

The After: The redesigned interface is on-brand and uses simple branching to help learners explore the specific behaviors that make someone a "successful wafeleur".

Image used with permission of Rimmer Creative Group

Text

In adding text-based content to your e-learning program, remember Mayer's "Select—Organize—Integrate" model discussed in Chapter 2. Provide clearly organized materials with strong headings and transitions, chunk material into manageable bites, and use plenty of white space. Also use text as a tool: employ bold, and color, and highlighting for emphasis (remember, though, not to overuse—the emphasis is lost when every other word is bold). Additionally, remember the two critical rules about using text in an e-learning program:

1. Cut it in half.

2. Cut it in half again.

Figure 4.24 shows an example of ruthlessly editing text.

Figure 4.24. Edit

BEFORE:
36 Words

> You make such decisions as which applicant to hire, what disciplinary actions to take if an employee breaks the rules, what information is recorded on the performance appraisal, who receives training and who gets the promotion.

AFTER:
8 Words

> ## YOUR CALLS:
>
> Hiring
> Discipline
> Performance Reviews
> Training
> Promotions

(An aside: We know from the research of Mayer and others that learning is enhanced if narration and on-screen text don't match. The first slide here might serve well as the voiceover to accompany the second slide.)

Lesson Learned

Use standard fonts. If you are distributing your e-learning program in a PowerPoint file format, unusual fonts may not display properly on learner machines.

Arial and Verdana are both readable non-serif fonts, and Times New Roman and Georgia are popular serif fonts. See the comparisons of 16-point fonts below, noting the difference in relative size and the space between letters:

Arial 16-point

Verdana 16-point

Times New Roman 16-point

Georgia 16-point

Take care using *italicized* text. It can be difficult to read, and learners may mistake it—and <u>underlined</u> text—for a hyperlink.

Chunk Content and Use White Space

Break content down into manageable "bites" for learners. Creating more screens is preferable to overloading fewer. This will reduce cognitive load for learners, thereby supporting the acquisition of new learning.

Next Stop: Creating and Editing Art

In creating effective e-learning from PowerPoint, be judicious in choosing meaningful art. The right image can illuminate, elucidate, and help to create the "ah-ha" moment that will make the online learning experience so worthwhile to learners. The wrong image, though—apart from being distracting—can actually hurt learning. The next chapter discusses ways of creating and editing art that will have an impact.

Creating and Editing Art

Now that we've taken a look at using graphics with meaning and text that supports learning, let's move on to actually creating and editing art. As we saw in the discussion of graphics with soul, the just-right image can make all the difference in making a program effective and engaging. Too many e-learning programs suffer from the dreaded "wall of words," due more to lack of creativity than lack of resources. PowerPoint itself provides means for creating and editing clipart, but it seems few users make much use of this capability. Additionally, the MS Paint program that loads with Windows (go to Start—All Programs—Accessories—Paint) provides additional capability at no cost. In this chapter we'll review some basics of creating our own art, editing existing art and photos, and saving images for use in our e-learning programs.

Bitmap or Vector?

There are two kinds of images: bitmap and vector. Bitmaps, also called rasters, are made up of pixels, or small blocks of color assembled to create the image. The icons on your desktop are bitmaps. As you can see from Figures 5.1 and 5.2, enlarging the image tends to distort it and make edges appear jagged. Although bitmaps are difficult to resize (going smaller gains considerably better results than enlarging), you may at some point find the need to work with them. Scanned images, images taken with digital cameras, and photographs, are bitmaps.

Vector images, on the other hand, are made up of what we might consider drawing objects. Lines, curves, and fonts are all vector graphics. Objects are resizable and retain their quality no matter how large. Figure 5.2 shows a simple vector image created with a PowerPoint Shape. Notice that enlarging it does not affect the quality: the outside line stays crisp.

Figure 5.1. Bitmap Images Are Made Up of Pixels

Figure 5.2. Enlarging a Vector Graphic Does Not Affect the Quality

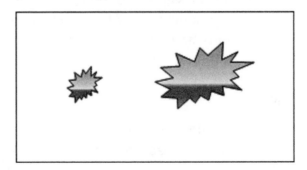

Because vector images are large filled blocks of color, they do not, however, display subtle shading or gradation well; for this reason, photographs do not work well as vector images, and it's why most clipart tends to look "cartoony." An advantage, though, to working with clipart vector graphics is that images can be ungrouped and edited individually; that is, each object in the clipart graphic can be enlarged, recolored, removed, duplicated, etc.

It's important to understand the basic differences between vector and bitmap graphics, as you will likely be working with both in the course of creating e-learning with PowerPoint.

Working with Shapes and ClipArt

Sometimes an idea can be very effectively conveyed with nothing more than simple shapes. Figure 5.3, uses PowerPoint Shapes to create an infographic.

Figure 5.3. Infographic Created with PowerPoint Shapes

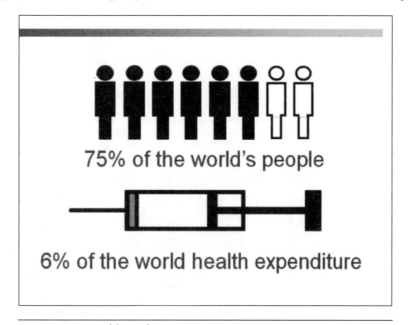

Source: Designed by Adam Warren

Designer Kevin Thorn (www.nuggethead.net), routinely uses PowerPoint shapes to create original images. This gives him complete control over placement and color.

Figures 5.4 and 5.5 show how he created an airplane and a notepad with pencil.

 See the website for more examples from Kevin.

PowerPoint allows you to move, recolor, crop, and make other changes to clipart and to photographs. Clipart images are vector graphics so can be modified in many ways. The next few figures were created entirely with clipart and PowerPoint Shapes.

 The website accompanying this book contains a tutorial on working with shapes, colors, and fills, and provides a narrated tutorial on creating the images in the figures below.

Figures 5.6 through 5.13 show how to build a complex learning image using PowerPoint shape and drawing tools. Instructions are contained on the figures here –as suggested by Mayer's theory—rather than written out in the captions below the figures.

Figure 5.4. Airplane Created with PowerPoint Shapes

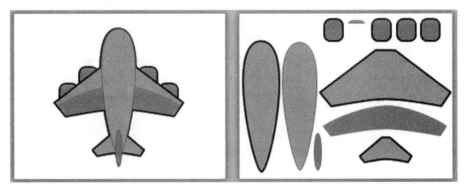

Figure 5.5. Notepad and Pencil Created with PowerPoint Shapes

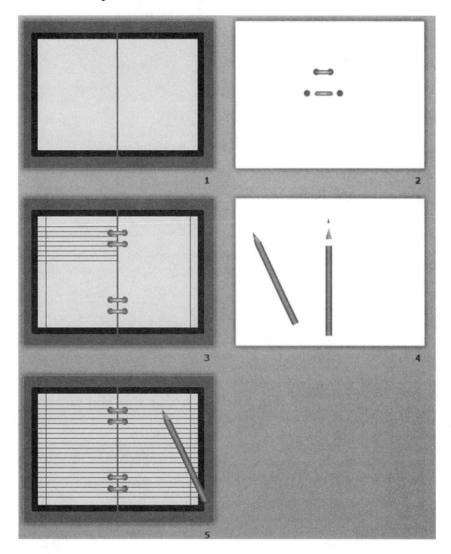

Figure 5.6. Begin with Shape and Drawing Tools; Draw a Hill

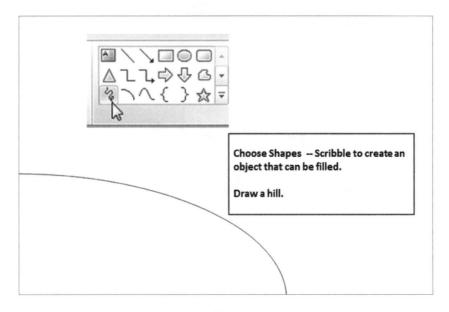

Figure 5.7. Color the Hill Green

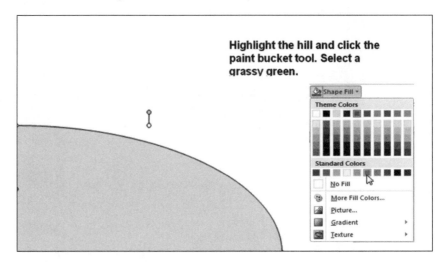

Figure 5.8. Insert Clipart Tree and Cloud

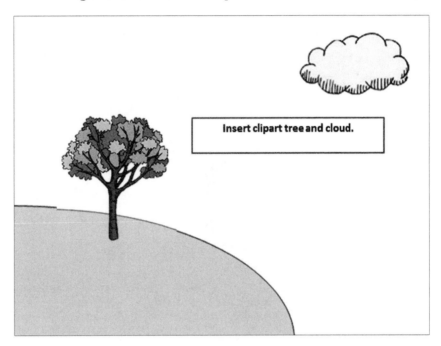

Figure 5.9. Add Water and Fill with Blue

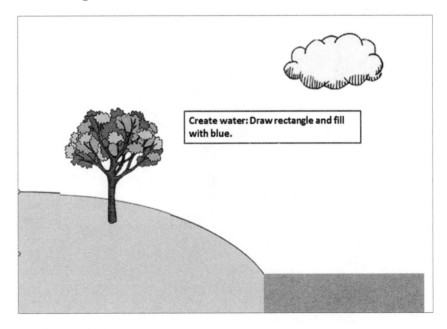

Figure 5.10. Send Water Back Behind Hill

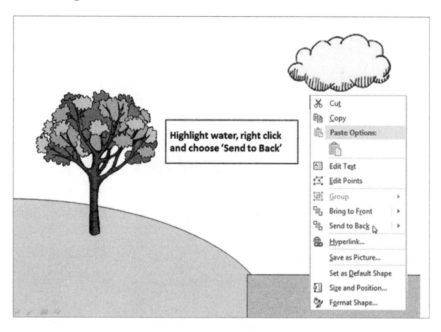

Figure 5.11. Create Condensation Lines

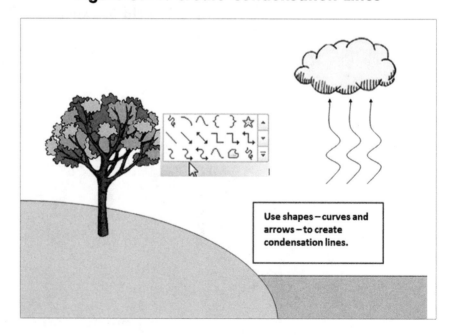

Figure 5.12. Create Waves

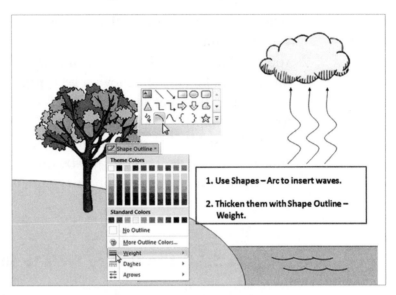

Figure 5.13. Completed Image

"How condensation works" material adapted from R. Mayer (2002). Cognitive theory and the design of multimedia instruction: An example of the two-way street between cognition and instruction. *New Directions for Teaching and Learning, 89,* 55–71.

Set Transparent Color

While most clipart from galleries comes with a transparent background, you may sometimes want to use a picture that has background included. You can remove backgrounds from many images using PowerPoint's picture toolbar. Figure 5.14 shows a key image that came with a white background; the designer wants to place this on a darker slide so needs to remove the white area from around the key image. To achieve the effect, choose "set transparent color," then click the tool inside the area you wish to change. This can also be used to remove backgrounds from photographs, as shown later in this chapter.

Figure 5.14. Use Picture Tools to Set Transparent Areas

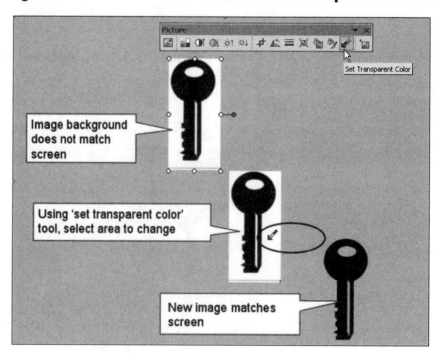

Transforming Clipart

The next example shows how to ungroup clipart to modify only segments of it. This allows you to, for instance, recolor segments or remove or add elements. The designer in this example has chosen to use a harvest metaphor for a program introducing learners to the basics of collaboration. A quick search of a clipart gallery for "farm" offers a number of choices. By clicking the gallery's link to "show by style" or "show all in this design," the designer can view all the available pieces of art with the same overall look and feel.

The designer likes the barn image (top center in Figure 5.15) but wants something in the foreground. She finds the image of a haystack (Figure 5.16) and wants to add several to the barn image, so needs to remove the rake. As this is a vector graphic, the components of the image can be ungrouped and individually edited (Figure 5.17). That is, each of the elements can be removed, resized, recolored, or otherwise modified, as seen in Figures 5.18, 5.19, and 5.20.

Figure 5.15. Farm Images from the Same Style/Gallery

Figure 5.16. Clipart Image of Haystack

Figure 5.17. Right-Click and Select "Grouping—Ungroup"

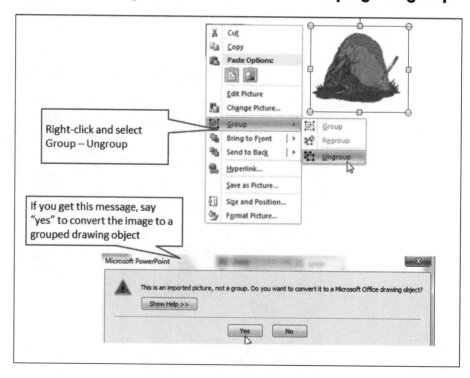

Figure 5.18. Editable Areas Will Appear. Regroup and Delete Pieces of Rake

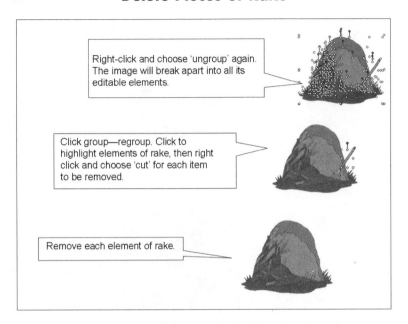

Figure 5.19. Create Copies of Haystack

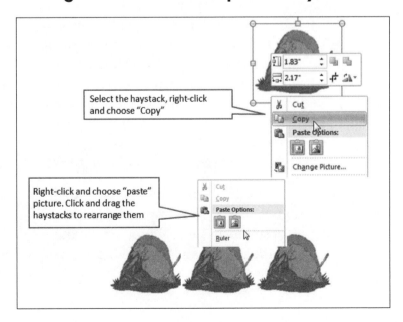

Figure 5.20. Copy Haystack and Paste onto Screen to Create Finished Image

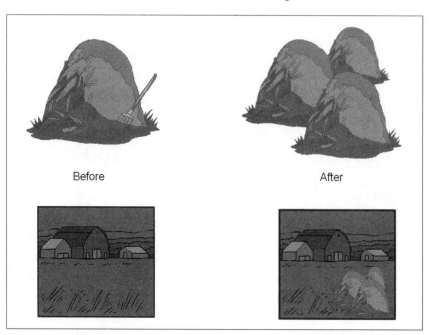

Once ungrouped, you can alter the colors in an image by clicking on the area to be recolored, then choosing the new color from "shape fill." PowerPoint 2013 introduced the new "Eyedropper" Color Picker tool (Figure 5.21), which gives designers greater ability to match colors in an image, and make for more even coloring of all images on a slide.

Is it e-learning, or is it just text information?

Just using "e-learning" as a way to deliver enormous amounts of text makes it very expensive in terms of time and effort and will result in an inferior product. If your e-"learning" program can be printed out as a Word document, then it should just be delivered that way.

Figure 5.21. Eyedropper Color Picker Tool

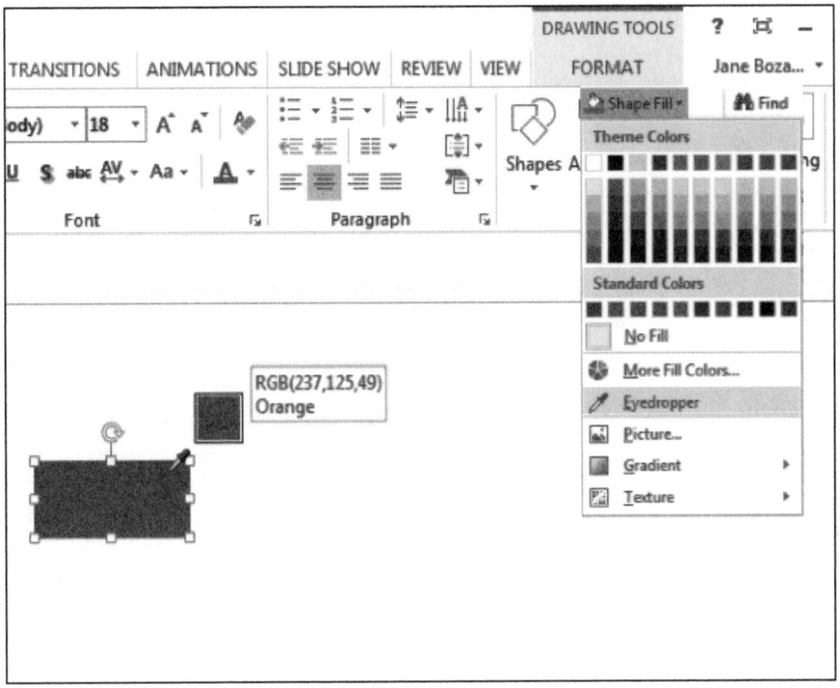

Editing Photos in PowerPoint

PowerPoint's picture tools offer many options for working with photographs as well as drawn images, from brightness corrections to saturation changes to resetting as grayscale and black and white. Figure 5.22 shows possible simple color changes to a photo; while you can't see it in the print version, there are many choices for applying different color washes. There is also an option for "artistic effects" so you can apply changes like paintbrush strokes, pencil-sketch effects, glow edge, and sponge painting effects. These can go a long way to improving ordinary or slightly imperfect images, and can help pieces of art from different sources or different styles appear more uniform. Figure 5.23 shows options for artistic effects applied to the clipart images shown earlier in Figure 5.8.

Figure 5.22. Options for Recoloring Image

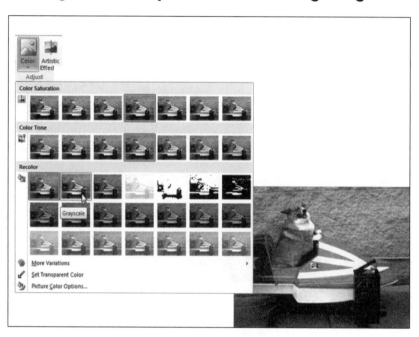

Figure 5.23. Artistic Effects Can Be Applied to Photos and Other Images

Photos can be enhanced by adding simple elements. The example in Figure 5.24, from a program on therapeutic restraints for clients in a residential treatment facility, shows PowerPoint circle and line added to highlight a section of the photograph. This allows the learner to see both the full position as well as the specifics of hand placement.

Figure 5.24. PowerPoint Shapes Emphasize Important Points of Photo

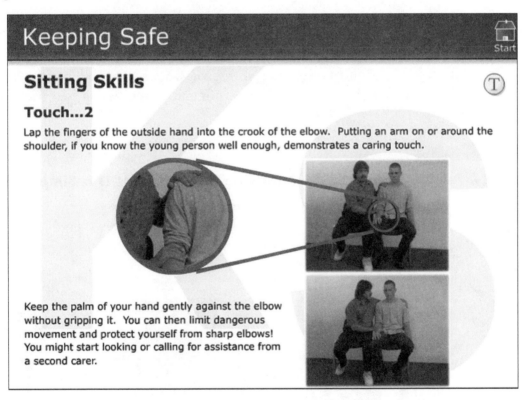

Photo courtesy of www.kwango.com

Removing Backgrounds from Photos

PowerPoint now offers a simple way to remove background textures, items, clutter, and other noise from photos, as shown in Figure 5.25. Insert the photo and click "Remove Background." The background of the image will turn purple. You can fine-tune areas you wish to remove and to keep. Once you click off the image, the background will be gone.

All Monitors Are Different

When testing your e-learning program, be sure to take a look at it on monitors other than your own. Colors, especially anything with subtle shading, may display differently on different screens.

Figure 5.25. Removing Backgrounds Is a Simple Task

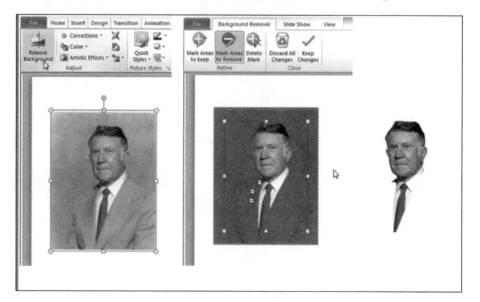

MS Paint

Occasionally you may want to make changes to an image beyond PowerPoint's capabilities. You may, for instance, want to add custom effects that are not offered by PowerPoint, to erase part of an image, or to work with a bitmap image.

You may not realize that you have access to a free graphics program, MS Paint, that is already loaded on computers with the Windows operating system. Click Start—All Programs—Accessories—Paint, as shown in Figure 5.26.

Paint comes with a number of tools for creating and editing art and photographs, as shown in Figure 5.27.

Figure 5.26. Paint Is in the "Accessories" Folder

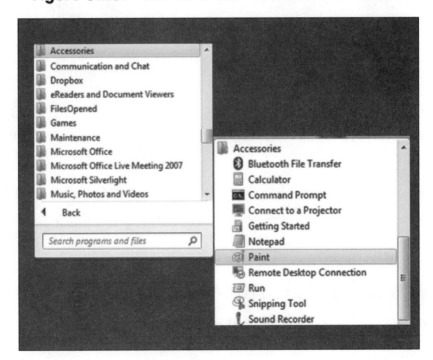

Figure 5.27. Tools Available in MS Paint

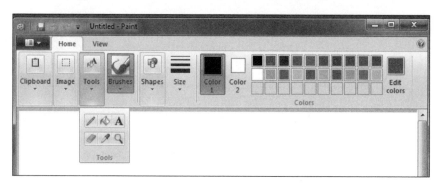

Figure 5.28. MS Paint Allows You to Edit and Customize Clipart

Ellipse Tool

Polygon Tool   Paintbrush Tool

Thanks to Alex Papadimoulis

Using Paint to Create and Edit Art

Figure 5.28 shows the effects you can obtain by applying different tools to the same clipart image.

Figure 5.29 shows how MS Paint was used to remove an object. Unlike the image of the rake in the "haystack" figures earlier (Figures 5.16 through 5.20), I found when I ungrouped this image that removing the man with the chainsaw would actually take away a large part of the tree trunk. So rather than use PowerPoint's ungroup feature, I instead used MS Paint's selection tool to outline the part of the image I wanted to remove, deleted the man with the chainsaw, then used the Color Picker tool to match the color, and finally the Paint Brush tool to repaint the missing part of the image:

Once the image is edited, copy and paste ("right-click—copy," "right-click—paste") to create an orchard or forest, as in Figure 5.30.

Figure 5.29. Use Paint to Remove Man with Chainsaw, Then Touch Up Area

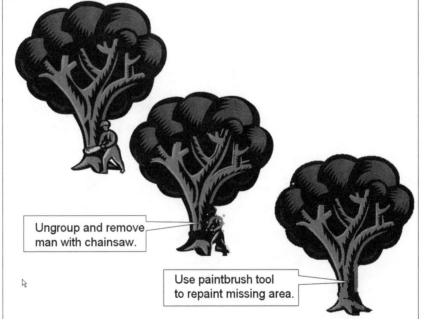

Figure 5.30. Edited Tree Copied and Pasted to Form Orchard

About Screen Shots (aka Screen Captures)

You can capture images of your computer screen, for instance showing your company's website home page, demonstrating an example in Excel, or illustrating how to access the MS Paint program, by using PowerPoint 2013's new "screenshot" capability: Insert > Screenshot. Some editing can then be done using the image tools.

The excellent "SnagIt" screen capture software from www.techsmith. com makes this task considerably easier, as it will let you select only the portion of a screen or image, then copy it, save it, add a border, etc. The newest versions include editing tools similar to MS Paint. SnagIt costs approximately US $50 and is a very good investment.

Editing Photographs with Paint

The Paint tools can also be used for editing photos. I wanted to use the image of a dog, taken on a child's ride-on toy in front of a department store, in a program I was working on. As shown in Figure 5.31, I used the selection tool to outline the coin box, the delete key to remove it, and then the paintbrush tool to recolor the lines on the area the coin box had previously blocked. Finally, I used the irregular selection tool to outline the dog and rocket, then the delete key to remove the background.

Figure 5.31. MS Paint Allows You to Edit and Customize Photos

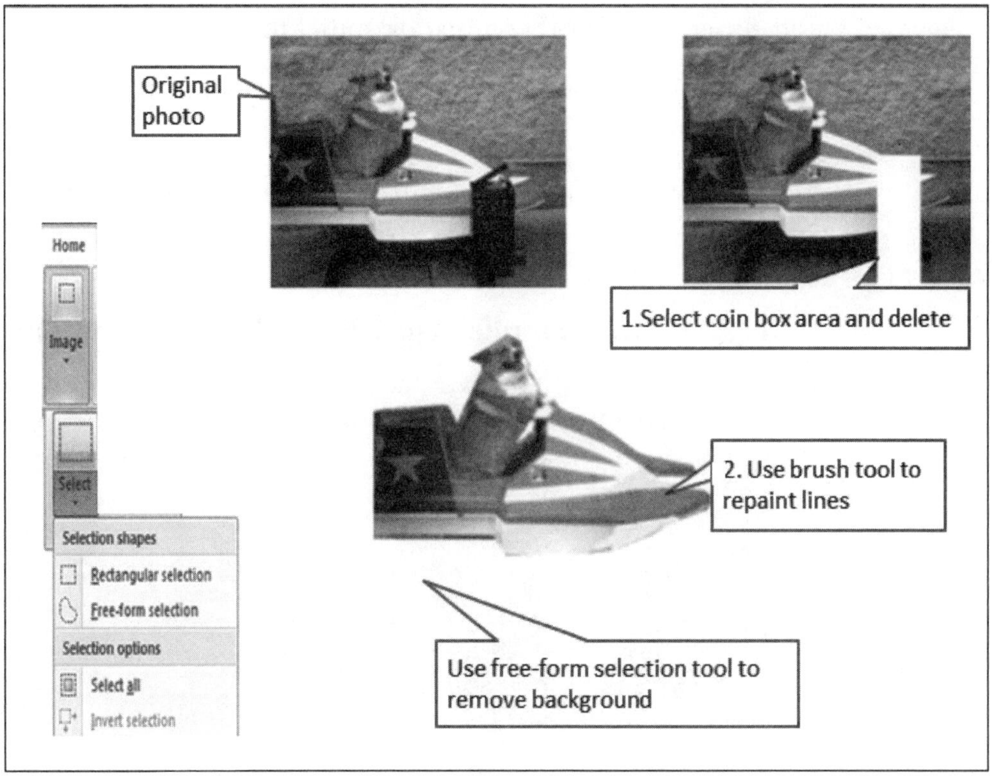

File Size: Compressing Images

A challenge in developing e-learning is being mindful of file size. The bigger the file, the more server space required, the more bandwidth necessary to distribute the file over the Internet to learners, and the slower the download time. In PowerPoint, the "compress picture" tool will reduce image size. Compressing photos does require some decisions on your part about what you consider acceptable for your project, as compression does reduce quality, as shown in Figure 5.32.

If using the "compress" tool from PowerPoint's Picture Toolbar (Figure 5.33), be sure to check the "delete cropped areas of picture" so the cropped parts will be eliminated rather than only hidden.

Images that are copied and pasted into PowerPoint are larger than those that are inserted. Save and label images, then use the "insert—clipart" and "insert—pictures" commands, rather than copy and paste images in.

When considering file size, consider your overall plan for your e-learning project.

Video, music, animation and narration also increase file size.

Figure 5.32. Smaller Files Show Reduction in Quality

175 KB   60KB   10KB

Figure 5.33. Compressing Pictures

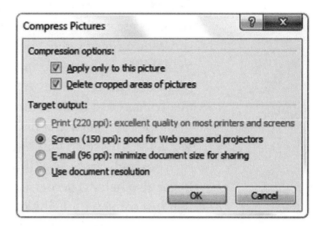

New Horizons

A big change since the publication of the first edition of this book has been the release of so many new mobile phones and other devices, many of them equipped with cameras supplemented by inexpensive photo apps. The creative designer is much less dependent now on commercial photography sites for material or what, in the not-so-distant past, would have been large and expensive resources like staff, cameras, lenses, and expensive editing tools.

New phone and tablet apps are being released all the time, so it's dangerous to bring up only a few here, but take a look at some especially well suited to instructional design work. Don't limit yourself, though: most apps are just a dollar or two and it's usually worth the time to download and just play with a variety to see what you can do. These are available for both iOS and Android operating systems; just search the

Internet for the manufacturer's sites. *Note:* Most are for use with touch screen devices so you may need to create them in one place and import them into your PowerPoint work.

Tools like Camera+ and Photogene are good all-around editing tools that can adjust image color and clarity, even adding a flash after the fact. ColorSplash turns a whole image to grayscale and lets you, with a finger swipe, bring back color of selected objects or areas. I have used this to show location of safety equipment in new-hire compliance training and to highlight important aspects of an image in a program on cognitive overload. Diptic is a way of assembling multiple images into something of a collage, useful in outlining before/after images or outlining, for instance, four steps in a process by arranging photos in a clockwise sequence. MySketch will transform a photo into pencil or charcoal sketches and can be useful in establishing a uniform look for all images. It can also help to de-personalize photos a bit, to ease the distraction that can come with using models who are recognizable company employees, as well as help to overcome problems when photos may be of less-than-perfect quality.

Next Stop: Animation

Making full use of PowerPoint's Shapes, drawing tools, and picture tools, supplemented with the MS Paint program, gives you considerable power in creating art that supports your instructional goals. Now that we've covered using graphics with soul, let's move on to creating animation that matters.

Animation

E ntire books are available on creating animations with PowerPoint. *This* book attempts to show how animations created with PowerPoint can support instructional objectives. A number of instructional animations are illustrated in this chapter and are meant as inspiration sources and idea-starters. With the advent of social and easier web tools, many people are generously sharing their animations, tricks, and tips. I am linking to a number of these on the book's website, but the public library is growing all the time. From time to time, especially when you're working on a project, try searching YouTube or the Internet for "PowerPoint animations."

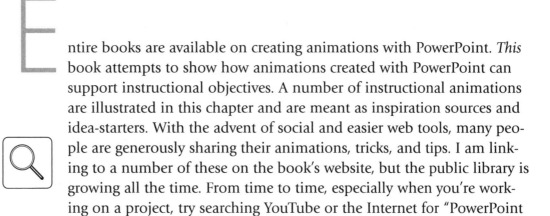

The website contains an "Animation Basics" narrated explanation and tutorial as well as working examples of many animations shown in this chapter. While developing skill at creating animations doesn't necessarily require a great deal of specialized training, it does require work, patience, a tolerance for trial and error, and possibly time spent in workshops and/or in reading instructional materials.

A great deal on the specifics of creating animation can be found by searching "creating animations with PowerPoint" or "animating PowerPoint." Whether live, by book, or online, though, the lessons will likely tell you how to use the animation features to do things like animate text or make pictures fly around. It will still be up to you to generalize that information to your ideas for creating effective e-learning. This chapter is intended to help you adapt these basic animations from entertainment to instructional purposes and provides an overview of animation basics, creating animations that teach, using animation to annotate graphics, using triggers to offer learner control over animation, and combining animations.

Animations can be applied to objects, photos, and text in several ways:

- Entrance—item appears on the slide

- Emphasis—may or may not involve motion; for instance, emphasis may involve changing color or size

- Exit—item disappears from the slide

- Motion Path—objects are set to move around the screen

Each of the animation effects is associated with variables: start (on click, on mouseover, per set timing), delay, speed, repeat, and trigger. The order of animations can be changed and can be set to include sound effects and narration.

Animation Should Support Instruction

Do not think of animation as an aesthetic concern—do not use it because you think it might make your presentation prettier or more engaging

**Rick Altman, President,
Rick Altman Digital Communications**

It's common to see PowerPoint shows with simple animations like fly-ing text and slide transitions. At best such animations draw learner eyes to a certain part of the screen; at worst, they are distracting and irritat-ing. Effective animation supports the instruction. Be sure the animations you use draw the learner's attention to important points rather than to whatever item happens to be moving, and don't overlook the value of changing colors and highlighting in focusing the learner's attention.

Animation Basics

Adding animation begins with selecting the object or text you wish to animate, then clicking "slide show—custom animation." Figures 6.1 through 6.8 show the basics. PowerPoint offers an array of animations, categorized as "basic," such as appearing, "subtle," such as fading, and "exciting," such as bouncing.

 About the animation files on the website: If you open these in slide show mode (View—Slide Show), you can see the animations work. Opening them as PowerPoint files—as if you were going to edit them—will give you access to the custom animation panel. Click the Animations tab. Open the Animation Pane to see how items on the slide were animated. (Figure 6.3 shows an open animation pane.) This is a good trick to use any time you have access to a PowerPoint file with interesting animations.

Figure 6.1. Select Object and Choose "Animations"

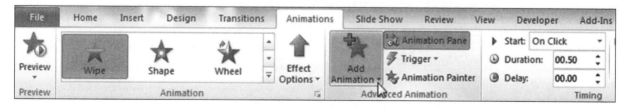

Figure 6.2. Choose Entrance, Emphasis, and Exit Effects

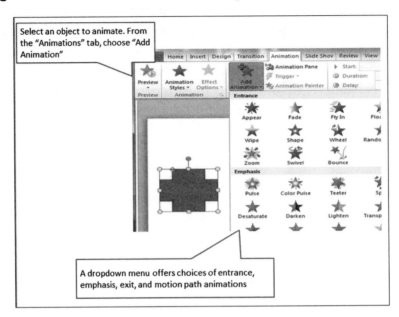

Figure 6.3. Animation Effects Are Numbered and Color Coded

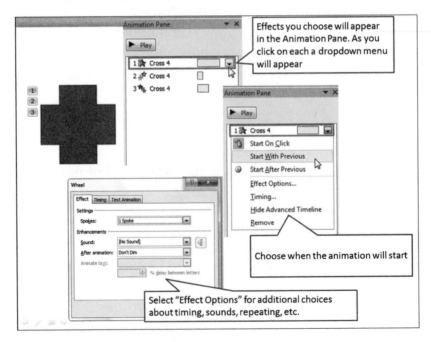

Figure 6.4. Array of Entrance Effects Available

Figure 6.5. Array of Emphasis Effects Available

Figure 6.6. Array of Exit Effects Available

Figure 6.7. Array of Preset Motion Paths. Custom Paths Can Also Be Drawn

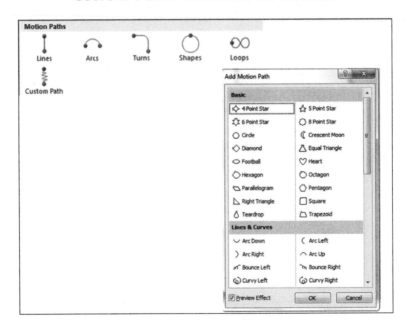

Figure 6.8. Set Timings for Animations

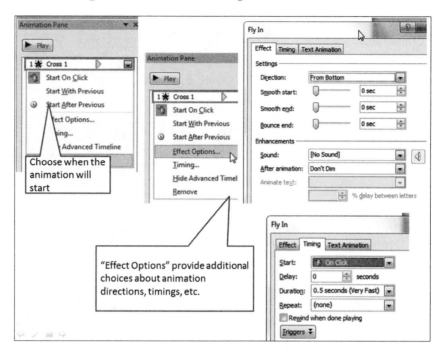

Animations That Teach

Some examples of animations that teach appear throughout the rest of this chapter. *Note:* For the purposes of illustration, this chapter shows a number of examples with transcripts of the narration added to the images. This is for the benefit of readers; the transcripts do not appear on the e-learning programs. The research of Mayer and others tells us that students learn better when animation and narration occur together rather than animation and on-screen text.

Process/Stages

Animation can illustrate processes, stages, or progression. In the "smoking" example shown in Figure 6.9, the name of each body part is

Figure 6.9. Animated Line Shows Smoke's Path

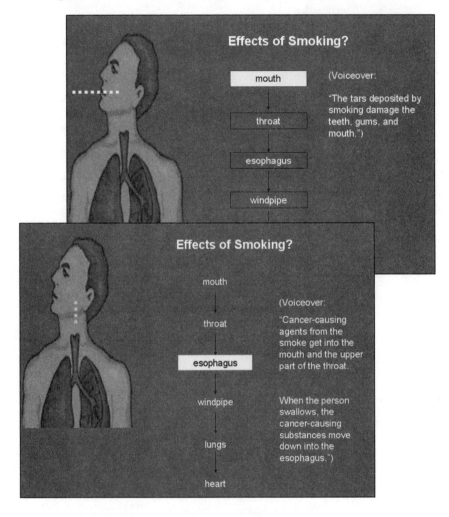

highlighted and explanatory text is displayed as an animated line moves from the mouth down into the lungs.

A working example of this animation is available on the website that accompanies this book. To see it work, open the file in Slide Show mode. To see how it was created, open it as if you were going to edit it, then click on "slide show-custom animation." The animation panel will open so you can see how the animation was created.

Demonstration

Animation can provide instruction in how things work. The screens shown in Figure 6.10 illustrate the concept of buoyancy in a submarine. The animation shows that as the submarine submerges the air chambers fill with water, weighing the submarine down. Submarine buoyancy concept and original images from www.onr.navy.mil/Focus/blowballast/sub/work3.htm.

In another example of demonstration, Figure 6.11 shows animation that illustrates how a simple pump works. As the pump handle moves down, pressure on the air inside forces the valve open and the air is pushed out.

Figure 6.10. Submarine Submerges as Air Chambers Fill with Water

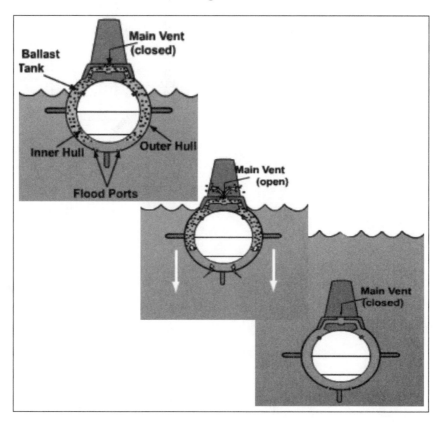

Figure 6.11. Animation Illustrates Working Pump

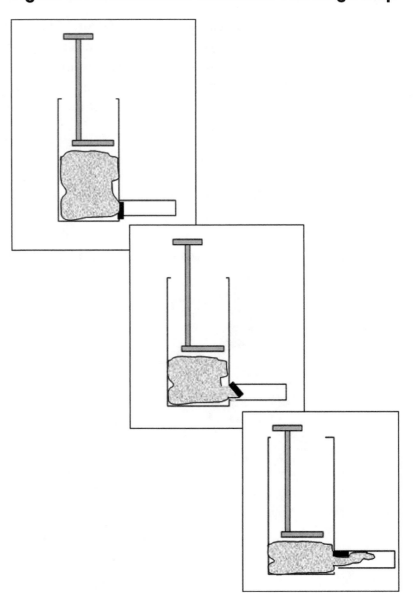

Realistic Movement

Flying, spinning text does not add to the learner's understanding. Use motion animations to illustrate, well, motion. Figures 6.12 and 6.13 both use "spin" animation to show the workings of things that spin or turn. The forklift image was created by combining the spin animation with a motion path to indicate forward motion. See pages 132 to 148 for more information on motion paths and combining animations.

Figure 6.12. Gear Spin Animation

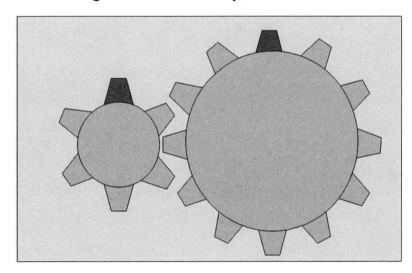

Source: Acadia Institute

Figure 6.13. Spin Animation Used to Illustrate Turn

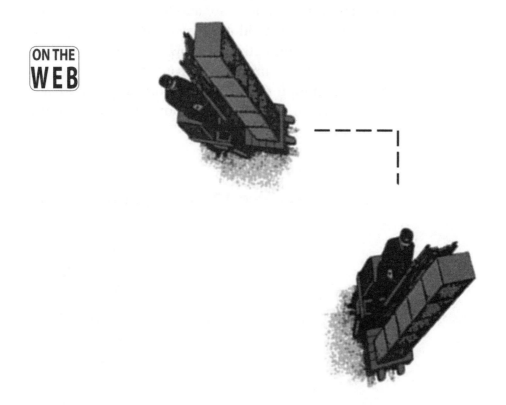

Order/Sequence

The introduction of motion path animations moved PowerPoint into real competition with higher-level animation programs. Figure 6.14 shows an example of a tutorial that uses motion path animations to teach sequencing in bagging groceries. Items appear to drop into the bag.

Figure 6.14. Motion Path Animation Allows Learner to See Order

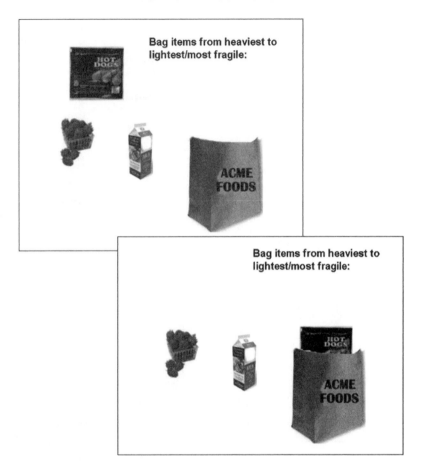

Figure 6.15 shows the motion paths. The hot dogs go first, followed by the milk and then the strawberries. By right-clicking each item and choosing "order—send to back" each item disappears behind the bag, giving the illusion of dropping inside.

Figure 6.15. Motion Paths for the "Grocery" Animation

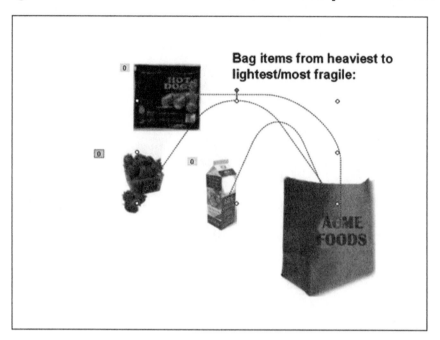

University of Toronto Professor Danton O'Day has written extensively on his experience in using PowerPoint to create animations for use in biology classes. Touting the quick development time and ease of use PowerPoint offers, O'Day frequently turns to PowerPoint for developing instructional animations. Search for "Danton O'Day PowerPoint" for links to his articles and interviews, as well as to working examples of animations he's created.

Charts, Timelines, and Diagrams

Animate charts to show changes, trends, information over time, or to explain difficult concepts. The example in Figures 6.16 and 6.17 show before-and-after approaches to animating a chart in an online "Aids Awareness" program. The slide's core message is that AIDS is on the increase. Notice how the right animation can support this message.

 A working example is included on the website.

Figure 6.17 shows the same slide with the template and text animations removed. The designer then emphasized the information that matters by using the "wipe up" command to animate the bar, illustrating the idea of increase.

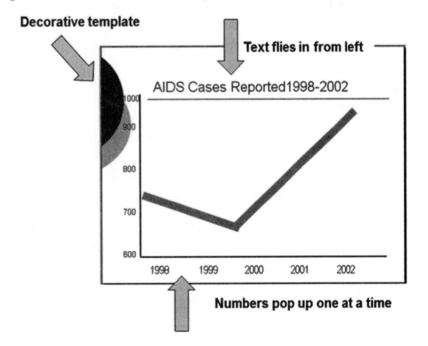

Figure 6.16. "Before" Image from Online AIDS Program

Figure 6.17. Important Information—the Increase in Cases—Is Animated

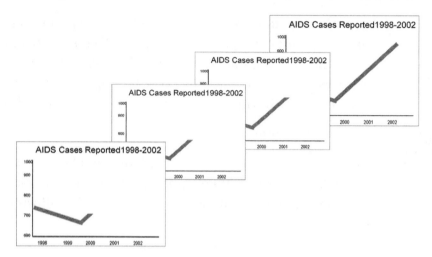

A working example of the chart shown in Figure 6.17 appears on the website in "Chapter 6—charts."

Figure 6.18 shows a company's expansion history. The heavy line marker moves across the timeline at the bottom of the screen as stars appear to show new units opened in a given year.

A challenge can be helping learners understand that processes in the "real world" often occur in fits and starts rather than in the smoothly outlined stages that often show up in manuals and memos. Figure 6.19 shows an animated timeline of the usual reality of the employee discipline process. The animation was created by using separate lines set to animate by wiping up, down, or right.

PowerPoint's animation features will allow you to animate parts of a chart; for instance, bars in a bar chart can appear in sequence or can climb, indicating growth. Pieces of a pie chart can appear in order, colors can change, etc. To animate the chart right click on it and select an animation; choose "effect options" to identify elements to animate. See Figure 6.20.

A working example of this chart is included on the website.

Figure 6.18. Animated Timeline

Franchise Expansion 2005-2012

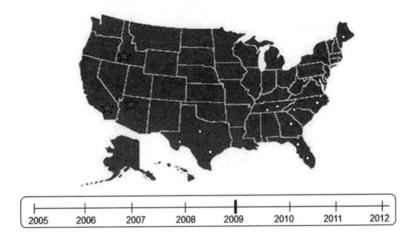

Figure 6.19. Animated Timeline Shows the Fits and Starts in a Process

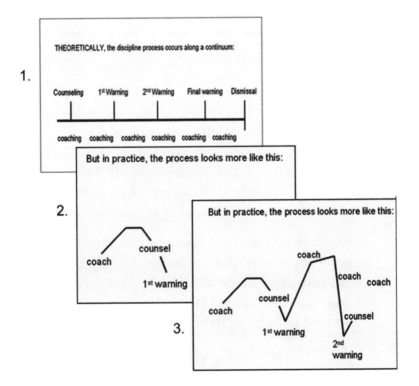

Figure 6.20. Chart Elements Can Be Animated Separately

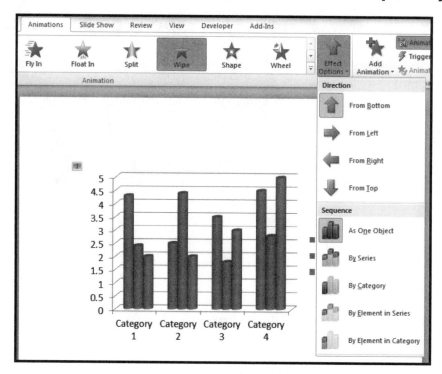

Using visual cues—such as animation or changes in color and shape—reinforce the message that an event has occurred.

> **L. Wilson-Paulwells. Bringing it into focus: Visual cues and their roles in developing attention.**
> *Journal of Biomedical Communication, 24,* 12–16.

Similarly, elements of a diagram can be animated. This can be used to show hierarchical relationships, stages in a process, levels of management in an organization chart, etc. Access the gallery via the "Insert—SmartArt" command. See Figure 6.21 for options available. Figure 6.22 shows how to animate items in a diagram.

Figure 6.21. Diagramming with PowerPoint

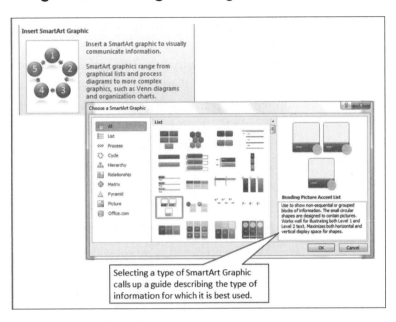

Selecting a type of SmartArt Graphic calls up a guide describing the type of information for which it is best used.

Figure 6.22. Animating a Diagram

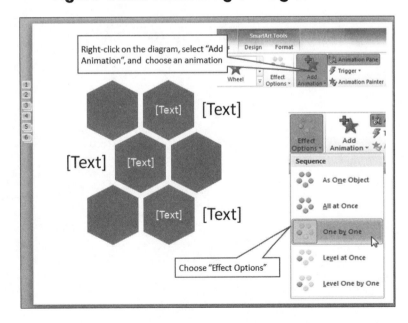

Right-click on the diagram, select "Add Animation", and choose an animation

Choose "Effect Options"

Annotating Graphics

While Mayer's research tells us to avoid substituting on-screen text for voiceover narration, animation can be used effectively to label or annotate a graphic with animated text or text boxes. Animating one item at a time (shown in Figure 6.23 by setting the text boxes to appear and disappear) minimizes the number of items on the screen, thereby reducing cognitive load, and allows the learner to see the whole image before text is introduced that might cover it.

Figure 6.23. Animation Can Be Used to Annotate Graphics

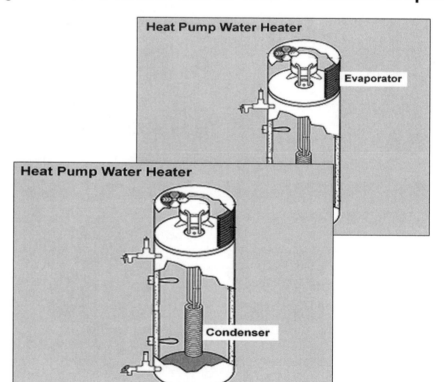

Providing Worked Examples

Research has shown that studying worked examples is often a more effective and efficient way of learning than solving conventional problems. Worked examples are also useful at reducing cognitive load and fits within Mayer's "SOI" model in helping the learner select, organize, and integrate new information. (van Gog, Paas, & van Merrienboer; Clark & Mayer; Clark, Nguyen, & Sweller; Mayer.) Worked examples can be particularly effective when providing instruction for novices. Figure 6.24 provides an illustration of an animated worked example. Text is animated a section at a time to show how the problem is "worked."

Figure 6.24. Worked Example of Applying Calculation to Problem

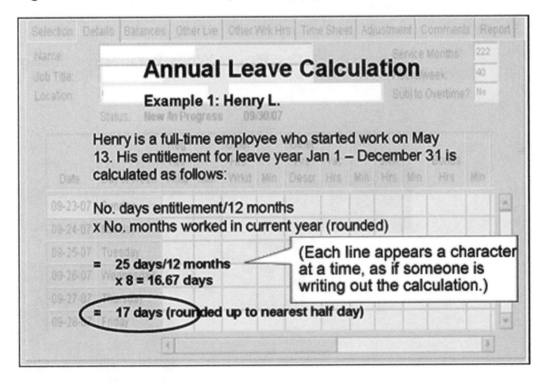

> Practice makes perfect: when you see an animation you like, try to figure out how you can create a "reasonable facsimile" of it with PowerPoint. You might be surprised at what you can accomplish.

Combining Animations

Combining animations can provide effects to rival that of more expensive and harder-to-learn software programs. The forklift example, above in Figure 6.13, was created by combining a curved motion path with a quarter-spin animation (so the forklift will turn while simultaneously moving forward.). In the animation shown in Figure 6.25, I want the car to move toward the learner. That's easy enough to create with a motion path animation, but I also need for the car to change perspective as it

Figure 6.25. Car Moves While Perspective Changes

Figure 6.26. Animation Settings for the Moving Car

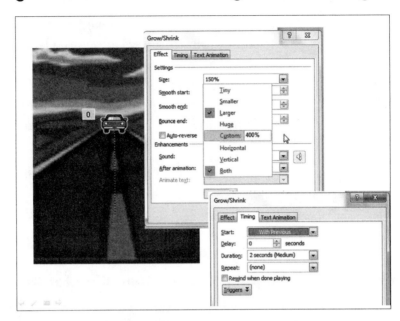

moves, appearing to come closer. By going to "Custom Animation—Add Effect—Emphasis—Grow/Shrink," and setting the second animation to occur "with previous," I can make the car appear to increase in size while simultaneously moving toward the learner. Figure 6.26 shows the custom animation panel for this.

 A working example of the "Car" animation is included on the website.

Practice

Developing skill in advanced animation techniques takes creativity, practice, patience, and, regardless of detailed instructions, some trail and error. You may also find alternate ways of achieving an effect or find some inspiration for a future project.

Trigger Animations

Where other actions we've looked at allow you to link a slide or object to another slide, a "trigger" allows the learner to start an animation, or sequence of animations, on a single slide. For instance, in the "gears" example first shown in Figure 6.12 above, a button can be added that would enable the learner to start the animation. Figure 6.27 shows the same animation with a trigger added; Figure 6.28 shows how it was created.

 A working example of the "gears" animation is included on the website.

Figure 6.27. Setting the Trigger Animation for the "Start Spin" Button

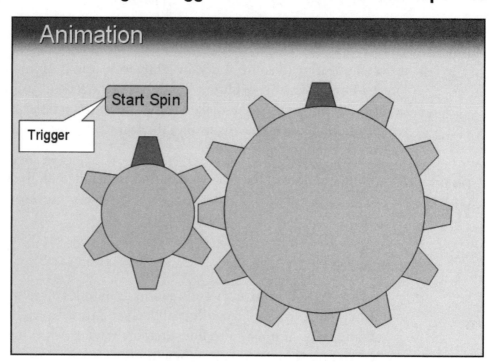

Figure 6.28. Choose "Effect Options" to See Choices for Setting Triggers

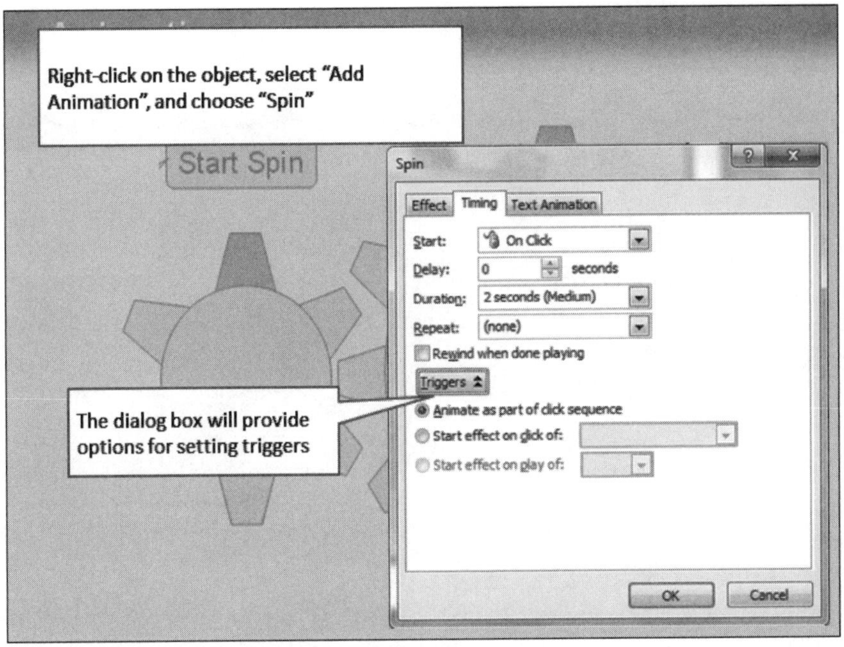

Triggers (Figure 6.29) can be especially useful when you want learners to control one or more animation sequences. The "submarine" example, originally shown in Figure 6.10, is designed to begin animating as soon as the slide loads. You could set the animation to start on mouse click and create a dummy button on the screen (any click will start the animation, but the button gives the illusion of a control button). With triggers, though, you could give the learner control like this.

The "grocery" example, shown in Figure 6.14 as an automatic animation, can be created with triggers. Learners would, upon clicking each item, start the motion path animation that moves each item to the bag. (*Note:* At this time, it is not possible to create drag-and-drop interactions in PowerPoint without learning complicated Visual Basic code. The animation shown in that figure is a reasonable substitute for a drag-and-drop interaction.)

Figure 6.29. Triggers Allow Learners More Control

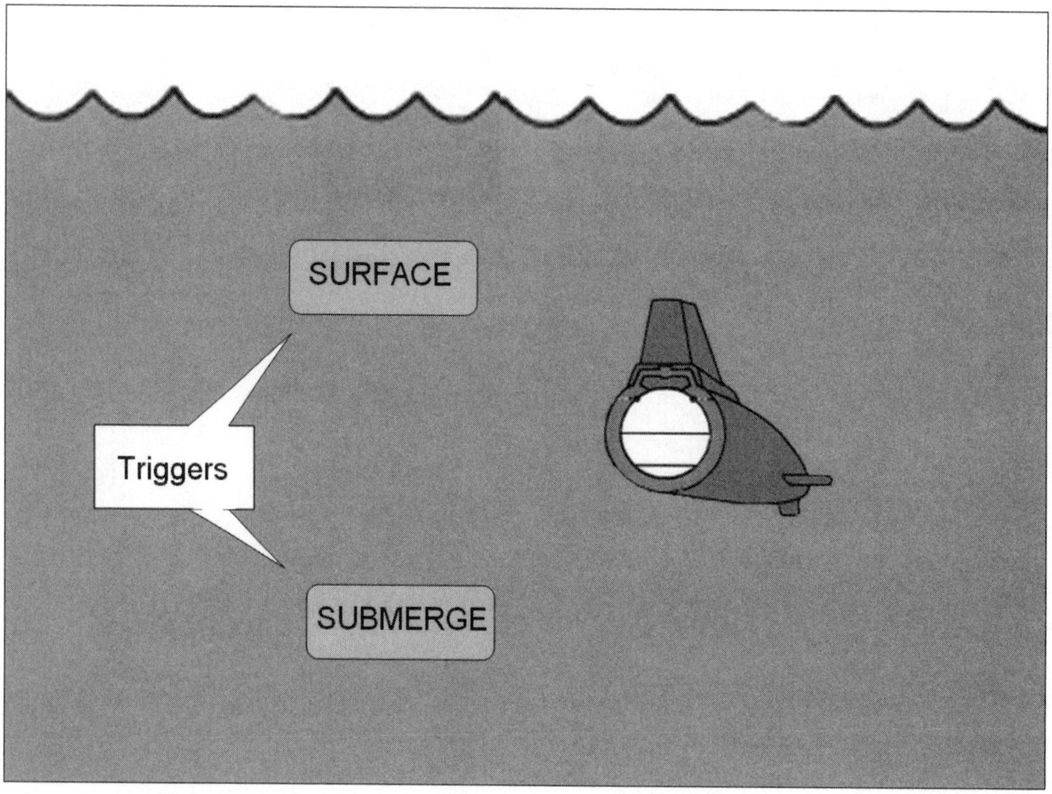

SURFACE

Triggers

SUBMERGE

Source: www.onr.navy.mil

Other uses of triggers include actions such as making quiz answers appear beside a question or provide ways of giving learners more control over content. An example is shown in Figure 6.30.

Figure 6.30. Clicking the Ovals Triggers Appearance of Explanatory Text

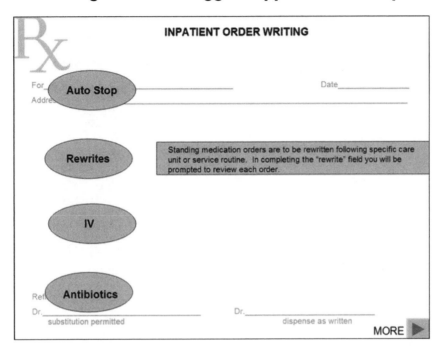

Next Stop: Interactivity

Animation, used with care, can help a designer move material from "content" to "instruction." It can help learners understand change over time, transformation from state to state, and illustrate processes. It can help learners select, organize, and integrate new learning and can reduce cognitive load. The next chapter shows ways of adding interactivity to PowerPoint-based programs to further draw in and involve the learner.

CHAPTER 7

Interactivity

t's unfortunate that so many e-learning programs take the form of screen-after-screen of content, serving as little more than "page turners." Clicking "next" is not interaction. A lot can be done with PowerPoint to build interactivity, from treasure hunts to interactive quizzes cast as game-show-type games. And, unlike paper-and-pencil activities, PowerPoint-based quizzes, games, and activities can be enhanced with graphics, visuals, and sound clips. It's important, though, to use interactivity thoughtfully and for the purpose of supporting instruction. Don't let the program become what designer Cammy Bean calls a distracting, pointless "clicky-clicky-bling-bling" experience. This chapter covers assorted strategies for encouraging learners to interact with e-learning programs in meaningful ways via quizzes, games, simulations, and interactive case studies.

The website accompanying this book includes working examples and detailed instructions for creating many of the items in this chapter.

The only appropriate exercises in an online learning course are ones that emerge directly from the objectives. Other questions and exercises might entertain learners, but because they do not directly relate to the objectives, they ultimately distract learners from the purpose at hand.

Saul Carliner, Assistant Professor of Educational Technology, Concordia University, and co-author of
Advanced Web-Based Training Strategies

It's All About Hyperlinking

Reminder: the crux of creating interactivity in PowerPoint lies with hyperlinking through mouse click or mouseover actions. The action takes the learner from one slide to another, or results in an some other "event"—a video clip plays, an animation sequence begins, etc.—caused by the learner's actions. There are several ways to create the hyperlinks:

1. Via a text link

2. Via an action button

3. Via an object, like a shape or photo, given an action setting

4. Via a "hotspot," an invisible action button placed over part of a slide or larger image.

Examples of these are shown in Figures 7.1 through 7.6.

Figure 7.1 shows an interaction created with action buttons that link to corresponding feedback slides. There are five slides associated with this interaction: The question slide, the slides corresponding to the three answers, and the "next" slide to which learners are sent upon completing the interaction.

Figure 7.1. Creating Hyperlinks with Action Buttons

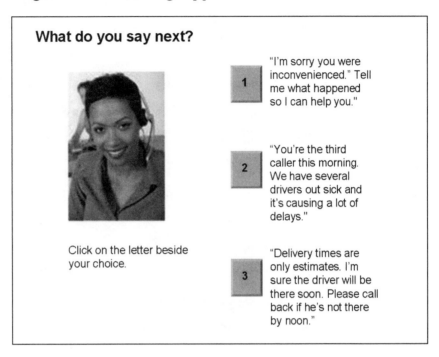

See the website for a narrated explanation of creating this interaction.

Hyperlinks can take many forms. While the slide shown in Figure 7.1 uses action buttons, you can also use letters (text), as shown in Figure 7.3, or objects such as boxes, as shown in Figure 7.4.

Figure 7.2. Text Hyperlinks to Corresponding Slide

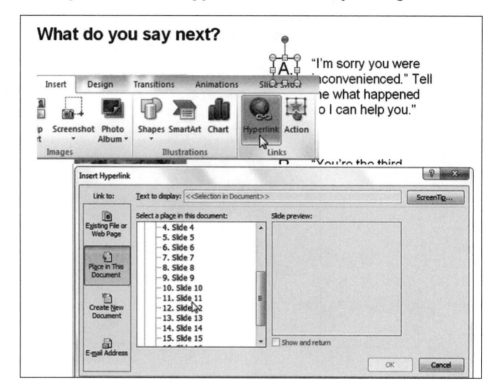

For setting hyperlinks from text or objects, first select the object, then right-click to access a drop-down menu. Choose "hyperlink." (You can also do this via the toolbar by clicking "insert-hyperlink".). Then choose the corresponding slide. This is shown in Figure 7.2.

Figure 7.5 shows the use of an invisible hotspot. Figure 7.6 shows how to create it.

Figure 7.3. PowerPoint Action Buttons Hyperlink to Corresponding Slides

What do you say next?

A. "I'm sorry you were inconvenienced." Tell me what happened so I can help you."

B. "You're the third caller this morning. We have several drivers out sick and it's causing a lot of delays."

Click on your choice.

C. "Delivery times are only estimates. I'm sure the driver will be there soon. Please call back if he's not there by noon."

Figure 7.4. Objects (Boxes) Hyperlink to Corresponding Slides

You chose:

"You're the third caller this morning. We have several drivers out sick and it's causing a lot of delays."

Click on the phone to listen to your customer's response to your choice.

What will you say next?

Figure 7.5. Invisible Hotspots Link to Corresponding Slides

Click the file cabinet to review background information, or click the door to let the client enter.

Figure 7.6. Creating a Hotspot

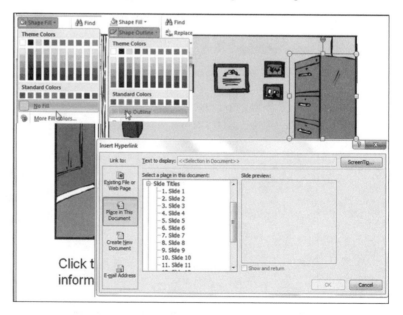

Hotspots in an image like the one in Figure 7.6 can be created by drawing a PowerPoint Shape over the object (in this case, a rectangle over the file cabinet), then create a link, as with the examples above. After the link is created, right-click and format the Shape (the rectangle) to 100 percent transparency and "No Outline."

Other actions can be assigned to objects. Figure 7.7 shows an example of an object set to play an audio clip.

Lesson Learned

When using invisible hotspots or buttons, be sure the invisible object is on top, or PowerPoint won't "see" it. Select the button or object, then right-click and choose "Order—Bring to Front" to ensure it's positioned on top of any other objects.

Figure 7.7. Object (Phone) Links to Voice Clip

Click on the phone to listen to your customer's response.

Levels of Feedback

The examples in the figures show simple interactions in which the learner chooses an answer and is taken to slides basically saying "right" or "wrong." Additional levels of feedback can be created through using additional slides. For instance, the first time the learner chooses the wrong answer the slide might ask him or her to "try again," pose the question once more, and again direct the learner to a second set of answer slides. If the learner again makes an incorrect choice, the corresponding slide might provide a hint, such as "that's still not right. Do you recall the limitations of the 'H' series printers?" and again pose the question. At the third incorrect choice, the learner might be advised to review material and return later. In this instance, there would be no "next" slide; the program would end there.

 See the website for a narrated explanation of creating quizzes with several levels of feedback.

Quizzes—Some Shaped Like Games

Basic Quizzes

The visual nature of PowerPoint lets the creative designer go from plain-vanilla paper-style quizzes to more meaningful learning activities, allowing learners to more closely connect content with application. Figures 7.8, 7.9, and 7.10 are some before-and-after examples.

Figure 7.8. Before: Text-Only Matching Quiz

Match the symptoms of aging to physical changes in the elderly.

a. cochlear degradation
b. loss of muscle mass
c. decrement in lingual sensitivity
d. decreased espophogeal motility

___1. indigestion
___2. loss of hearing
___3. loss of balance
___4. loss of taste

Figure 7.9. After: Matching Quiz with Images

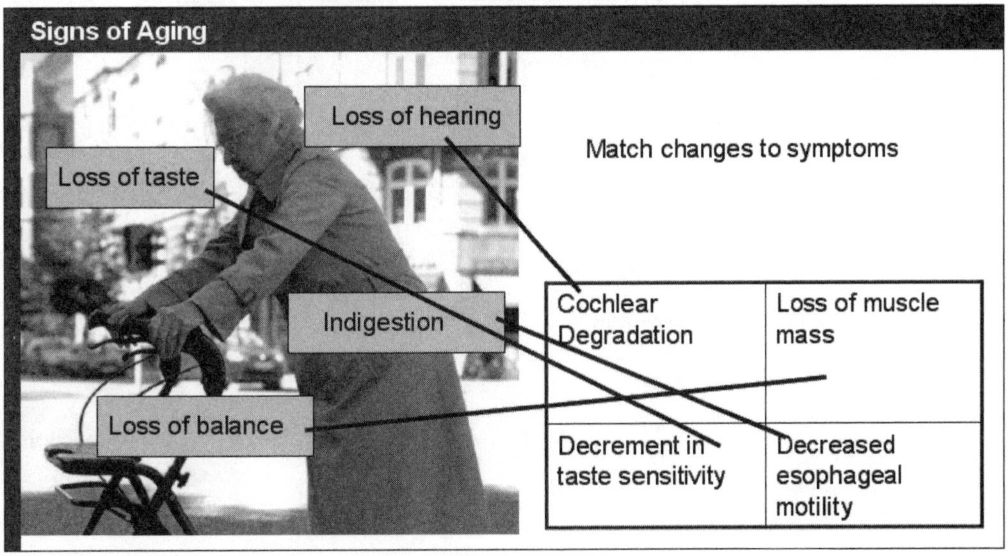

Signs of Aging

Loss of hearing
Loss of taste
Indigestion
Loss of balance

Match changes to symptoms

Cochlear Degradation	Loss of muscle mass
Decrement in taste sensitivity	Decreased esophageal motility

Figure 7.10a. Before: Text-Only Multiple-Choice Quiz

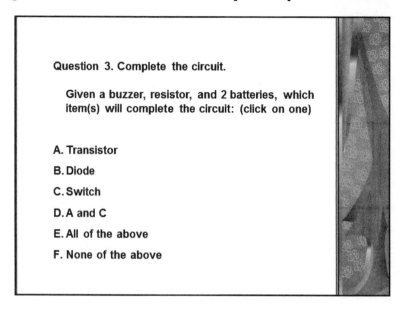

Figure 7.10b. After: Multiple-Choice Quiz Using Images

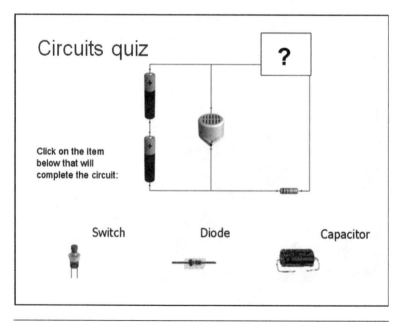

Source: Simon Drane; component images from www.crocodile-clips.com

> ## "Active" ≠ "Busy"
>
> Richard Mayer (see Chapter 2) reminds us that effective instruction engages the learner's mind and encourages him or her to think. Simply being physically active—like clicking "next"—does not support transfer or retention of new learning.

Types of Quizzes

It is critical that learners be provided with frequent opportunities to assess and, if necessary, correct, themselves. Familiar quiz formats, such as matching, word search, true/false, and multiple choice, are easy to create with PowerPoint. While "training" should be more focused on performance of a task or behavior, many topics do require learning things like definitions, names of machine parts, or points of a policy. Those of us charged with creating learning experiences on such things can find it very challenging to make it interesting for the learner. An activity like "Jeopardy" can be a good way to review a lot of content without simply listing it or offering it as a long series of questions. Below are photographic examples of some quiz formats, with brief information about how they were created.

Matching

Figures 7.11 and 7.12 show two different ways of setting up matching exercises: the first with connecting lines, the second with numbers.

Figure 7.11. Matching Exercise

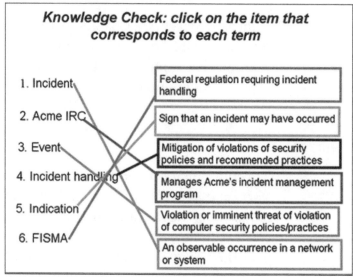

Courtesy Marirose Coulson and Donna Ebling, Booz/Allen/
Hamilton

Figure 7.12. Matching Exercise

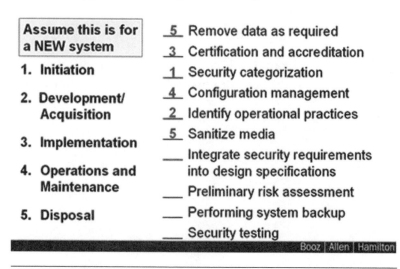

Courtesy Marirose Coulson and Donna Ebling, Booz/Allen/Hamilton

Figure 7.13. Set Items to Appear on Click

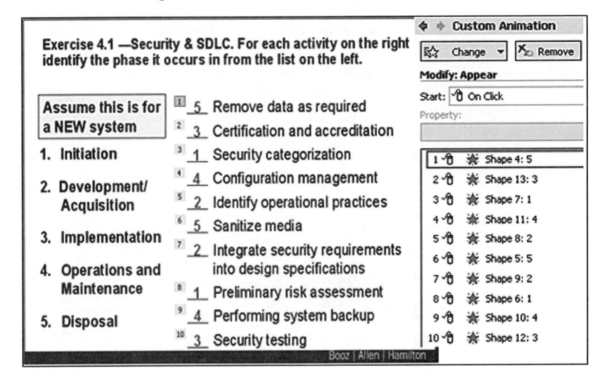

To create this, use custom animation to set numbers (or lines) to appear on click. An illustration is shown in Figure 7.13; a working example of these matching exercises are included on the website accompanying this book. The interaction could also be created by inserting action buttons and setting triggers for each matching event.

Lesson Learned

When creating slides with multiple linked textboxes and objects, take care to ensure that areas given hyperlinks don't overlap.

Figure 7.14. Example of True/False Quiz

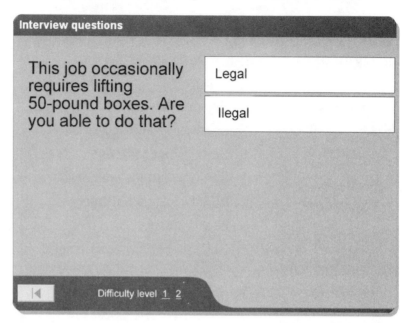

True/False

True/false is really just a single choice between two items, as shown in Figure 7.14. Each choice (legal or illegal) links to a corresponding answer slide. Some other substitutes for "true/false" choices are "yes/no," "agree/disagree," and "fact/fiction."

The example on the website "Create Interaction," while specific to Figure 7.1, shows the same technique used in creating true/false items.

Multiple-Choice and Game-Show

Although most people probably have never noticed, television game shows often take the form of multiple-choice quizzes. Using a game-show format provides learners with what e-learning expert William Horton calls "a seductive test." While we can debate the value of such testing, the fact is that many compliance courses come with an implicit requirement that a learner memorize material or somehow "prove" that he or she understands things like definitions and facts to show successful course completion. Game-show formats are familiar to learners so there is usually little time needed for understanding rules. Also, try to be creative: Don't just think of quizzes as testing recall only. With some creativity, you can formulate questions that require application and evaluation of content and move beyond the "seductive test" level. Some examples are shown below.

The example on the website "Create Interaction," while specific to Figure 7.1, shows the same technique used in creating multiple-choice items.

Figure 7.15. Multiple-Choice Quiz

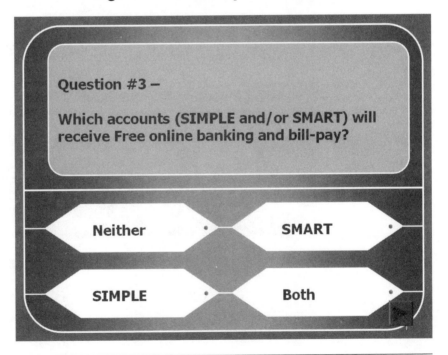

Thanks to Kathy Keller

Figures 7.16 and 7.17 show a game-type variation on the multiple-choice quiz, this one regarding diversity issues from Kwango.com. Learners are presented with an example of a problem situation and asked to choose the type of discrimination. Each character is covered with an invisible action button; on mouseover more information appears about the character's opinion. Learners then click the character to select their answers.

Figure 7.16. Diversity Challenge Question and One Character's Opinion

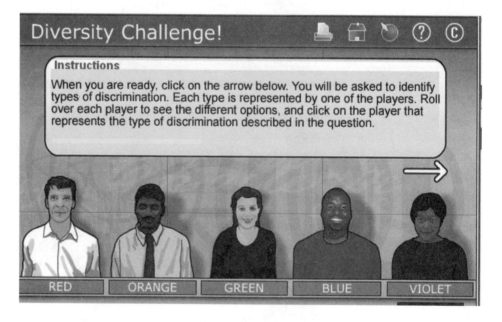

Figure 7.17. Another Character's Opinion

Jeopardy-Type

Jeopardy-type quizzes are an excellent way to review material or deliver a good deal of new information in a way perhaps more interesting than straight presentation of content. Figure 7.18 shows a Jeopardy-type quiz used in an online program on troubleshooting skills for heat and air conditioning repair technicians. Each button on the main board links to an answer slide, which in turn links to the question slide, which has a link for returning back to the main board. (Remember, in Jeopardy the learner is presented with the answer first and then has to ask the question.)

Figure 7.18. Jeopardy-Type Quiz

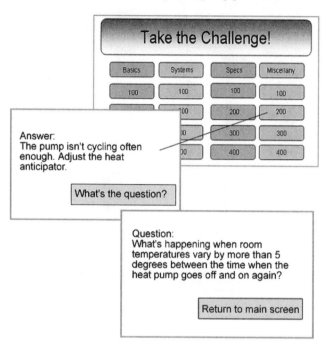

 The website includes a template for a Jeopardy-type quiz called "Challenge Board."

Pyramid Games

Similar to Jeopardy, the pyramid (shown in Figure 7.19) offers learners categories, which in turn lead to questions. This example is from a program on sales techniques.

Figure 7.19. "Pyramid" Quiz

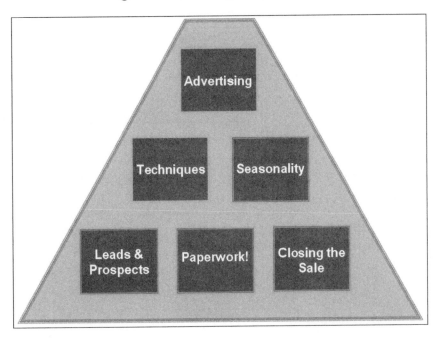

The website includes a template for a "Pyramid" quiz.

Hollywood Squares Games

This is another variation on the multiple-choice approach, with characters asking questions to which the learner is asked to respond. Variations of this (like the one in Figure 7.20) could include audio clips of the characters asking questions (Figure 7.21) or photos of real company "characters" (HR Director, Benefits Rep, Shop Foreman, etc.) instead of clipart images.

Figure 7.20. Sample Squares Game Board

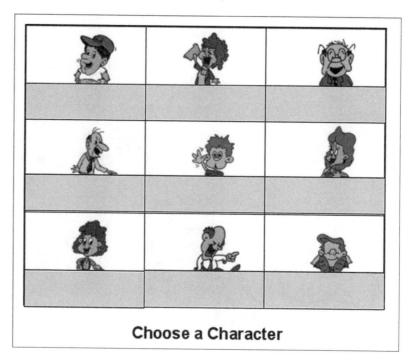

Choose a Character

Figure 7.21. Sample Squares Question

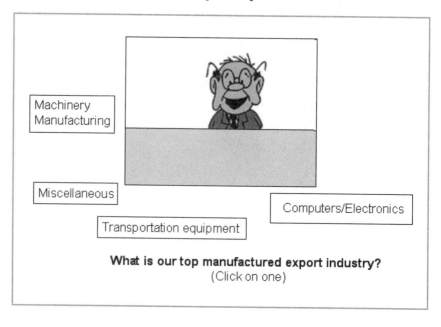

"Millionaire" Games

Figures 7.22 and 7.23 show a multiple-choice quiz designed to resemble the "Who Wants to Be a Millionaire?" game show. As with the TV version of the game, options exist for choosing hints and reducing the number of choices by selecting "50/50."

The 50/50 option hyperlinks to a slide with two choices removed.

Figure 7.22. "Millionaire" Quiz with Hints

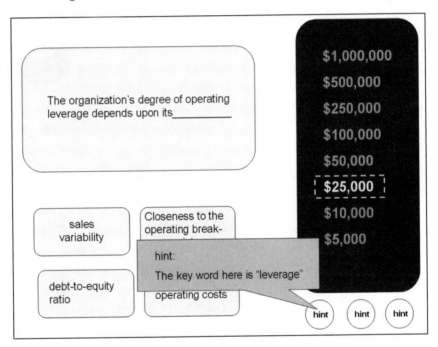

Figure 7.23. "50/50" Option Takes Away Half the Choices

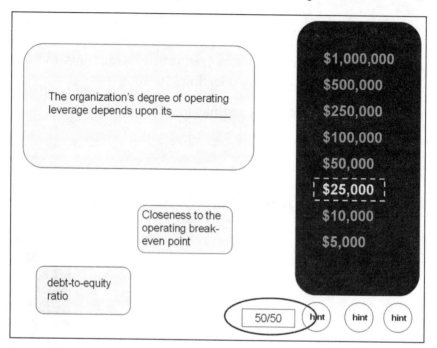

 The website includes a template for a Millionaire-type quiz.

(*Note:* You probably know that there are often more ways than one to achieve a particular effect in PowerPoint. The examples for adding the hints and 50/50 option to the "Millionaire" game are shown in the figures using hyperlinks to additional slides. They could also be created with trigger effects: animations would take place on one slide rather than linking to others. The choice may depend on your plans for distributing the program to your learners. At this time, trigger animations do not work reliably in some PowerPoint-to-Flash converter products. Personally, for an activity like this, I find it easier to create multiple hyperlinked slides than work with a sequence of animations on one slide.)

Lessons Learned

When using quizzes, be sure to give learners access to the correct answers! For instance, use feedback slides ("Sorry, the correct answer is B") or use hyperlinks to direct learners back to reference material.

Timed Quizzes

There are several ways to add an element of timing to PowerPoint-based quizzes. The easiest: set slides to advance after a given period of time, as shown in Figure 7.24. You can also add a running timer, clicking off seconds or other increments, by creating one slide per time frame (one per second, per 15 seconds, etc.). Both of these would lend themselves nicely to a virtual flash-card activity. It's also possible to add a running clock–type timer to the screen.

Figure 7.24. Setting Up Timed Quiz; Slide Advances After Ten Seconds

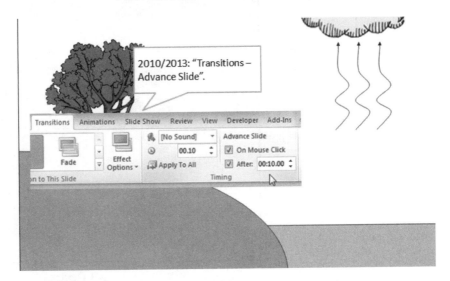

Timed Photo Reveal Quiz

Figures 7.25 shows a screen from a visual recall quiz for machine field repair staff. Each slide contains a decreasing number of color blocks. Slides are set to advance every five seconds, and point values decrease as additional information is revealed.

Running Timer

Quizzes can be set up so that the learner sees a countdown in time increments. This is done by creating a separate slide for each time frame (in the case of Figure 7.26, one per second); then slides are set to advance in accordance with that time frame. *Note:* This can become very cumbersome. While you can copy and paste the question text from slide

Figure 7.25. Photo Reveal Activity. Point Value Decreases as More of the Image Is Revealed

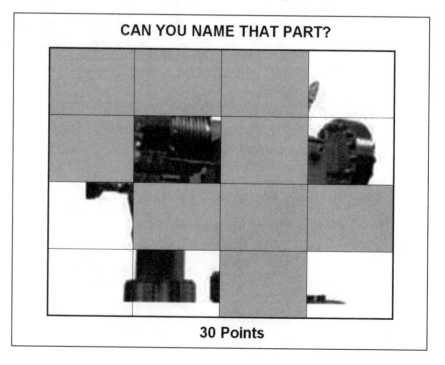

Figure 7.26. Timer Changes with One Slide Per Second

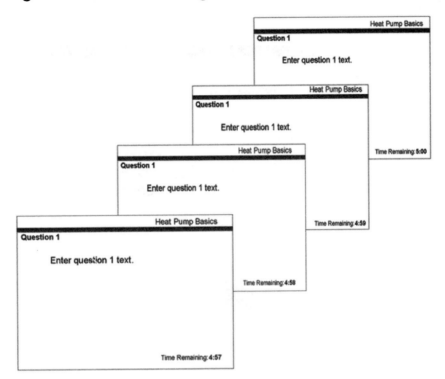

 to slide, you will still have to go in and manually enter the time on each slide—and counting down a minute by seconds means editing *sixty* slides. If you really want to do this, try searching for "PowerPoint timer." You will find some add-ins and templates you can download and edit.

Another way of creating a running timer is by inserting a small clock or counter on the slide. Figure 7.27 shows a timer created by animating pieces of a pie chart to appear every ten seconds. The slide then advances at the sixty-second mark.

Figure 7.27. Clock-Type Timer Used in a Quiz

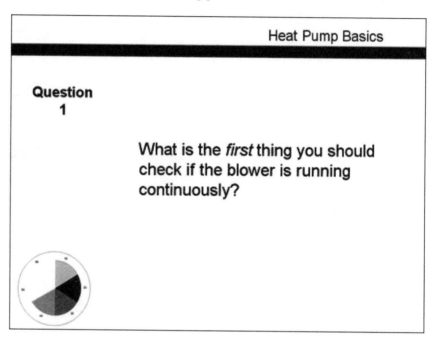

Board Games

The board game format is also an option, as shown in Figure 7.28, the home screen from "Bacteriopoly." Players begin with 100,000 bacteria; the object is to reduce this as much as possible. While this was originally designed as a classroom team game for use in schools, I recently repurposed it with some updated graphics for use in a "lab safety" refresher program for adult learners. The squares on the board hyperlink to corresponding slides. The original game is available in an editable form via Ferl; just search for "Bacteriopoly."

Figure 7.28. "Bacteriopoly" Game Board

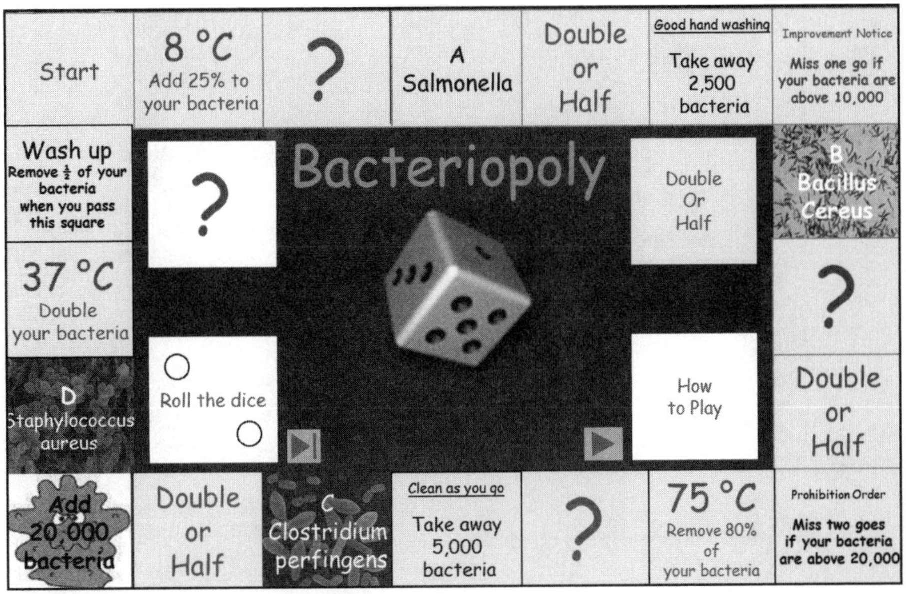

Thanks to designers Martyn Hulme and Jon Kent

Linking to External Games and Quizzes

Want more? It is an easy matter to insert a hyperlink from your
PowerPoint program to an external quiz or game. The lowest-level example would be linking to a Word- or Excel-based quiz. For higher-level
interactions, inexpensive (ranging from free to under $100/year for a
subscription) game and quiz engines can simplify the creation process
and can offer some activities difficult or impossible to create with
PowerPoint, like fill-in-the-blank quizzes. Figure 7.29 shows a
PowerPoint screen with a hyperlink to a quiz created with a commercial
Flash game template. This quiz is from Quia, a company that offers
many easy-to-use game and quiz templates *and* hosts them on their own
servers. You create the item, then Quia stores it and provides you with a
link to it. See also Figure 7.30, a link to an online game.

Figure 7.29. PowerPoint Linking to External Quiz

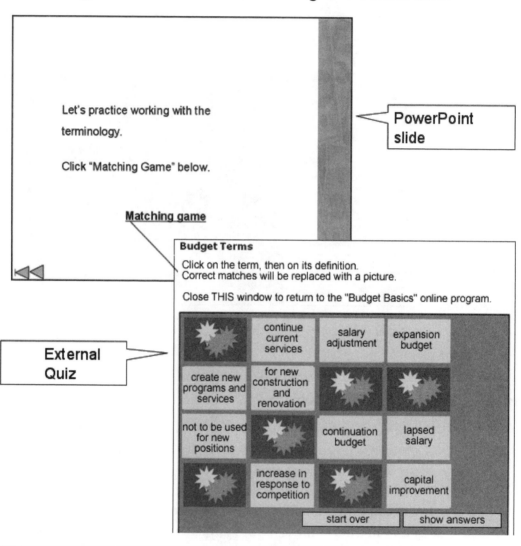

Thanks to Quia (www.quia.com)

Figure 7.30. A Hyperlink from the PowerPoint Slide to the Online Quiz

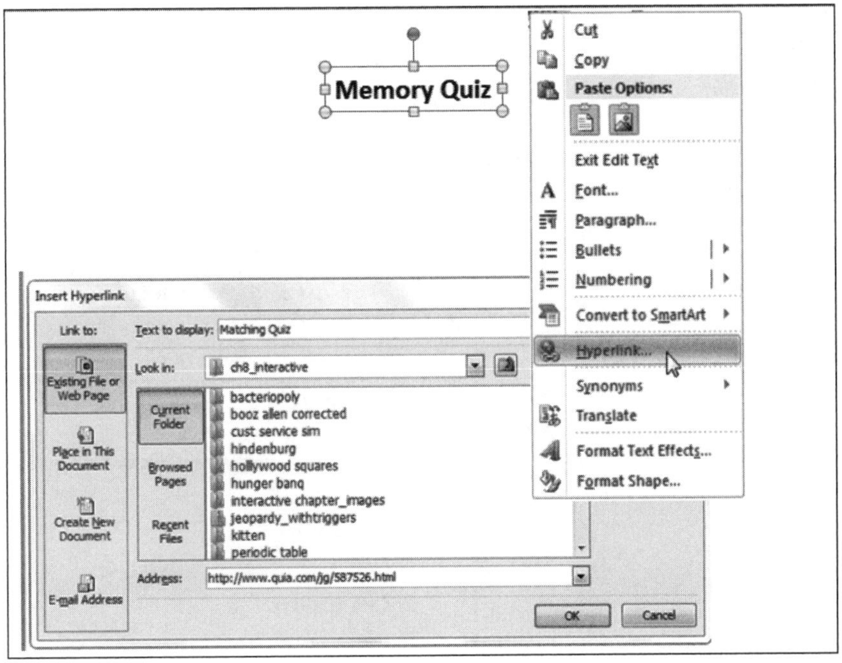

Need to track test scores? You can link from your PowerPoint slide to externally hosted quiz or online survey engines (search for "quiz engines"). Figure 7.31, an example created in minutes with an online template from Quia, shows a link to an online test along with one of the accompanying score reports available (Figure 7.32). Figure 7.33 is the "trouble spots" report, which points out any learners who are having trouble, or indicates questions that may be problematic.

Figure 7.31. PowerPoint e-Learning Program Links to Online Quiz

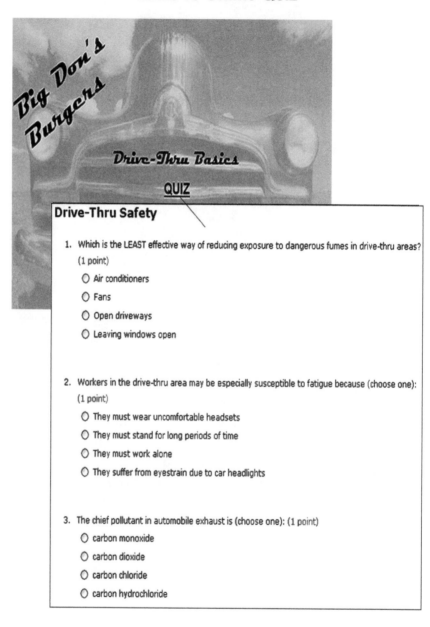

Figure 7.32. Example of Feedback Provided to Learner

Drive-Thru Safety

Thank you. Your responses have been computer graded. Here are your results.

Score Summary		points earned	points possible
(Click on question number to jump to question.)			
Question 1	correct	1	1
Question 2	incorrect	0	1
Question 3	correct	1	1
Question 4	correct	1	1
	Score: (75%)	3	4

1. Which is the LEAST effective way of reducing exposure to dangerous fumes in drive-thru areas?

   • Air conditioners
   • Fans
   • Open driveways
   • Leaving windows open (correct answer, your response)

   Points earned: 1 out of 1

2. Workers in the drive-thru area may be especially susceptible to fatigue because (choose one):

   • They must wear uncomfortable headsets
   • They must stand for long periods of time (your response)
   • They must work alone
   • They suffer from eyestrain due to car headlights (correct answer)

   Points earned: 0 out of 1

3. The chief pollutant in automobile exhaust is (choose one):

Figure 7.33. "Trouble Spots" Report, One of Several Reports Available

Trouble Spots Report

Activity: Drive-Thru Safety

QUIA

Overall Summary

Low Score	High Score	Mean	Median	# of Students
2 (50.0%)	3 (75.0%)	2.75 (69.0%)	3 (75.0%)	4

Students who scored zero or who started but did not submit answers

None

Students who scored 70% or less

Student Name	Points (out of 4)	Percentage
Diamonds, Carol	2	50%

Questions answered correctly 70% of the time or less

Question	Average Score	Number of Times Received
1. Workers in the drive-thru area may be especially susceptible to fatigue because (choose one):	0%	3
2. Workers in the drive-thru area may be especially susceptible to fagtigue because (choose one):	0%	1
3. Which is the LEAST effective way of reducing exposure to dangerous fumes in drive-thru areas?	67%	3

About Quia

For those on tight budgets—and even those who are not—Quia (www.quia.com) is an excellent all-around quizzing and tracking tool. A corporate subscription is only $199 per year and offers access to Flash game templates for several different types of quizzes, surveys, score reports, feedback to learners, and even class web-page hosting. It is hosted on Quia's servers, so no downloads are required, and—this is important—you can deploy activities to *unlimited* users. While it was developed for use by school teachers, I know a number of private organizations and government agencies using Quia to support workplace training efforts.

Simulations

Simulations ask the learner to perform a skill in some sort of context. The example of bagging groceries using trigger animations first shown in Chapter 6 (and repeated in Figure 7.34) provides learners with a simulated task.

A more common type of simulation involves branching decision making as learners move through a series of problems. These types of interactions can be quite powerful, as learners can see the consequences of their actions. Creating good simulations is a matter of choosing realistic situations and sketching the "branching" that the simulation will

Figure 7.34. One Type of Simulation Provides Practice with a Task

Figure 7.35. Decision Tree for a Simple Simulation

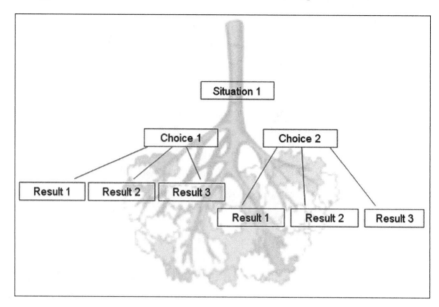

require. As with creating quizzes, it's a matter of laying out a series of "if-then" statements, followed by "and then," "and *then*." The simulation will involve branching decision making; you may have seen this represented as a decision tree. Figure 7.35 shows the layout of a simple simulation. Boxes represent separate slides.

Simulations are instructionally powerful, as learners experience the consequences of their own actions and decisions. While they can become quite elaborate and intricate, their success depends on careful planning—in the laying out of the decisions and results—more than on technical skill.

Figures 7.36 and 7.37 show a sample from a PowerPoint-based customer service simulation. The learner chooses a role, is presented with a problem situation, then receives feedback.

Figure 7.36. Choice of Role

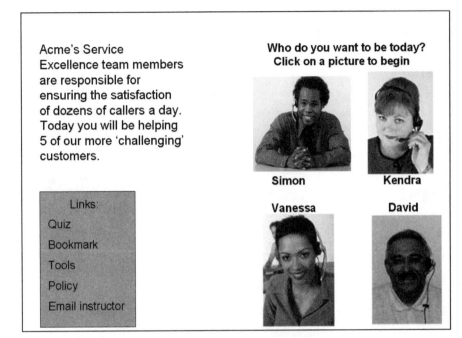

Acme's Service Excellence team members are responsible for ensuring the satisfaction of dozens of callers a day. Today you will be helping 5 of our more 'challenging' customers.

Who do you want to be today?
Click on a picture to begin

Simon   Kendra

Vanessa   David

Links:
Quiz
Bookmark
Tools
Policy
Email instructor

Figure 7.37. Presentation of Problem

Click on the phone to hear
what the caller has to say.

Figure 7.38. Learner Presented with Choices and Result of Decision

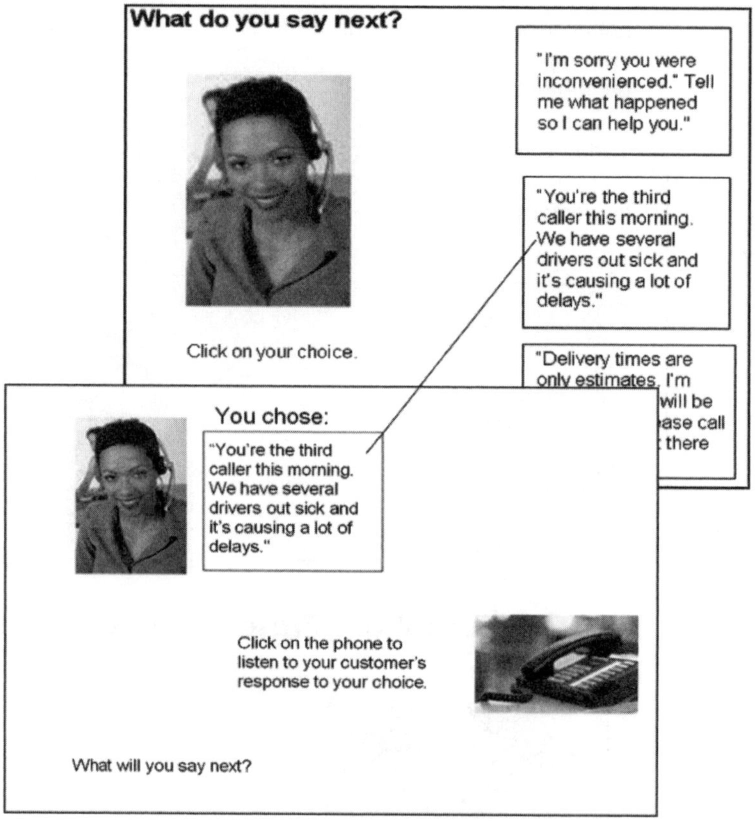

This customer service simulation is especially strong due to the addition of "customer" voice clips (see Chapter 10 for instructions on adding voice clips). Figure 7.38 shows another screen from the customer service simulation. The learner has chosen a reply that only escalates the situation. Clicking the telephone plays an audio clip of an angry voice saying, "Every time I call I get more excuses from you people. If I'm the third caller, then why isn't someone already working on this?! I am SICK of all the problems with deliveries!" Again, a good simulation lets learners experience the consequences of their actions.

Figure 7.39. Simulation Showing Email Interaction

```
EMAIL

To:    CustServ@abc.com
From: FrankL@symp.net
Subject: NO DELIVERY!!

I am FED UP with your delivery department's
inability to ever keep any promises. As usual,
the shipment arrived 2 weeks late. You say the
fifteenth, but you mean the first. WHY don't
you just say the first in the first place!

                                        Click on the best response:


TO: FrankL@symp.net                 TO: FrankL@symp.net
From: Vanessa@abc.com               From: Vanessa@abc.com
Subject: NO DELIVERY!!              Subject: No delivery

I can see that you're upset about this.    Mr Lyons,
Delivery times are only estimates. I will  I regret that you've been inconvenienced
forward your comments to the shipping      and I want to help. Let me make sure I
 department so they will be more careful   understand: you were promised delivery on
next time.                                 the 15th and you did not receive the product
                                           until the first of the following month. Is that
                                           correct?"
```

Figure 7.39 shows another screen from the same simulation, this one asking the learner to respond to an email complaint.

Figure 7.40 is the decision tree from another simulation, "Hindenburg's Dilemma," for use in online leadership training. Hindenburg's choice of reactions to the new constitution leads to still more decisions or undesirable consequences.

Figure 7.40. "Hindenburg's Dilemma" Provides Choices and Consequences

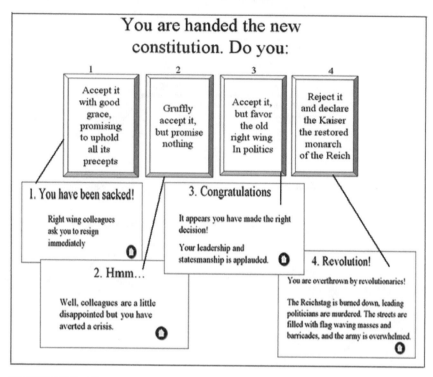

"Hindenburg's Dilemma" is used with permission of creator Rob Johnson; you can see the full program at http://ferl.becta.org.uk/display.cfm?resID=5023

Figures 7.41 and 7.42 show programs created by the Royal Veterinary College. The is from the "Emergency Case Simulator," in which veterinary students are presented with a case and must choose from possible actions/treatments set as hotspots across the bottom of the screen. This simulation is especially noteworthy for providing realistic practice with a critical task, minimizing the costs—both monetary and other—associated with the topic, and confronting learners with the ultimate consequence: death of the pet. The program can be accessed at http://www.rvc.ac.uk/Review/Cases/Index.htm.

Figure 7.41. Icons Hyperlink to Choice of Actions

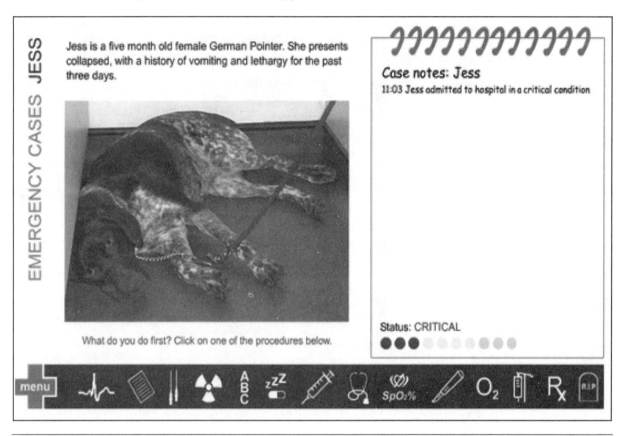

Source: Royal Veterinary College

Figure 7.42. Screen from "Gamekeeper's Conundrum" Simulation

The Gamekeeper's Conundrum

"Can I use levisol in partridges?"

You phone your colleagues for advice. Whose do you take?

Source: Royal Veterinary College

Another online course from the Royal Veterinary College, "Gamekeeper's Conundrum," is shown in Figure 7.42. Part of a series called "Pitfalls in Practice," this is an ethics program developed in response to negligence claims filed against veterinarians in their first year in practice. Each photo links to a text slide of "advice" from the person chosen. Note the use of simple photos with Shape callouts and text at the bottom of the screen. It's available online at www.rvc.ac.uk/Review/Pitfalls/pitfalls.htm.

Case Studies and Stories

Cliff Atkinson, author of *Beyond Bullet Points*, speaks of the importance of developing a strong story. Use of characters, plot, and a good story-line can provide compelling learning: think of good storytellers you know. Screens from Eduweb's online program, "A. Pintura: Art Detective" uses the theme of a *noir* movie mystery to take learners through a tour of art history. The scenario uses the characters of A. Pintura: Art Detective, and the distraught client Miss Featherduster to build a story around the mystery of a painting found in an attic. The designer uses this as a clever launching point for taking learners through an overview of art history and comparison of several painters. Along the way the learner has considerable choice about what to view, and in what order. The material is used with permission of Eduweb and has been slightly modified for the screenshots here (Figures 7.43 and 7.44). The program can be accessed at www.eduweb.com/pintura.

To ensure that my point here is not lost: there are a thousand ways to present information on art history that are not interesting or engaging. This designer found a way to make it quite compelling.

Again: It's about design, not software.

Figure 7.43. Setting and Introduction of "A. Pintura: Art Detective"

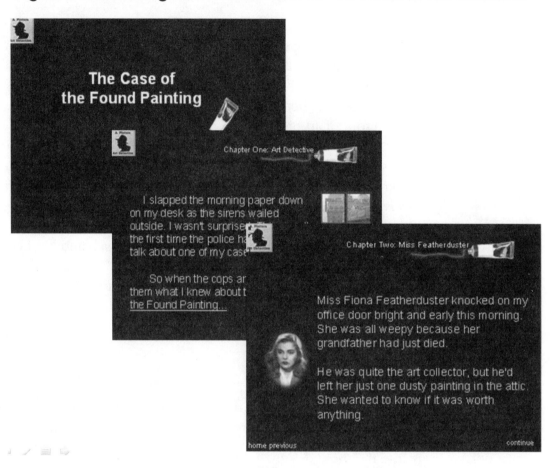

Used with permission of Eduweb

Figure 7.44. Comparison of Found Painting to a Raphael

Used with permission of Eduweb

After choices in navigating, learner arrives at a comparison of found painting to a Raphael.

Figures 7.45 and 7.46 show screens from another interactive online experience, the "Hunger Banquet" case studies. The program is available in full at www.hungerbanquet.org. Learners are offered a choice of characters, provided with scenarios from the character's daily reality, and then asked to make choices about actions to take. This program is created entirely with photographs, simple images, and hyperlinks. As with the "A. Pintura: Art Detective" program shown earlier, the designers of HungerBanquet found a way to make dry factual and statistical information engaging and compelling.

Figure 7.45. One Case from www.hungerbanquet.org

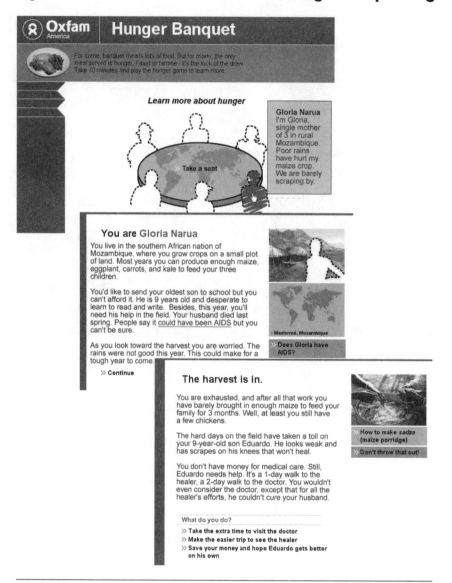

Used with permission of OxFam

Figure 7.46. Continuation of the Case

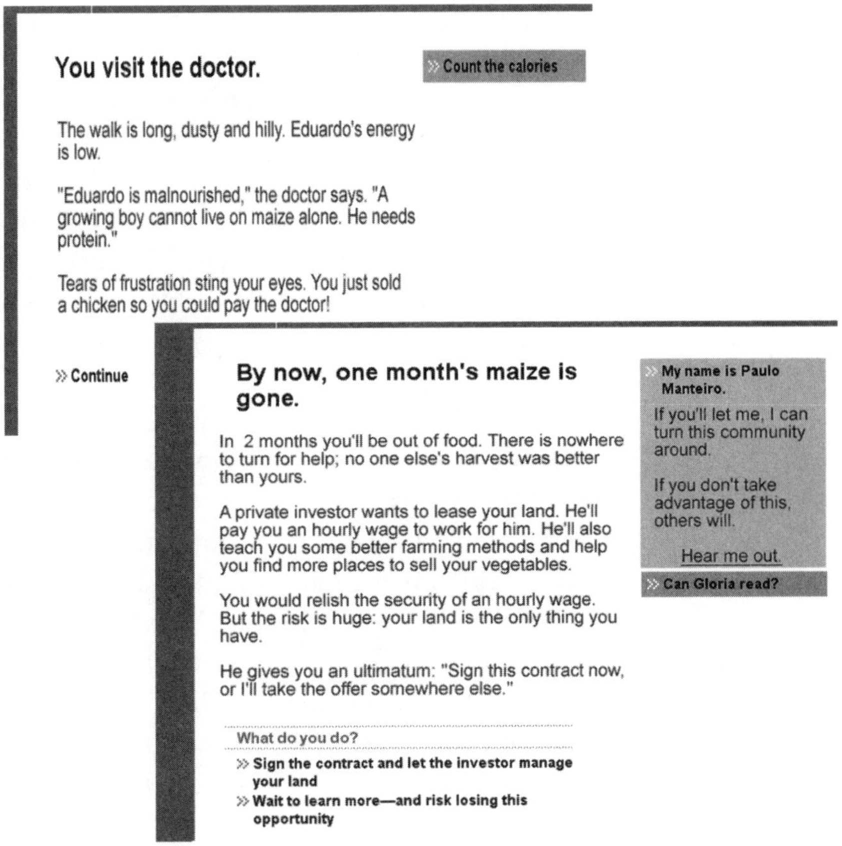

You visit the doctor.   » Count the calories

The walk is long, dusty and hilly. Eduardo's energy is low.

"Eduardo is malnourished," the doctor says. "A growing boy cannot live on maize alone. He needs protein."

Tears of frustration sting your eyes. You just sold a chicken so you could pay the doctor!

» Continue

By now, one month's maize is gone.

In 2 months you'll be out of food. There is nowhere to turn for help; no one else's harvest was better than yours.

A private investor wants to lease your land. He'll pay you an hourly wage to work for him. He'll also teach you some better farming methods and help you find more places to sell your vegetables.

You would relish the security of an hourly wage. But the risk is huge: your land is the only thing you have.

He gives you an ultimatum: "Sign this contract now, or I'll take the offer somewhere else."

What do you do?

» **Sign the contract and let the investor manage your land**
» **Wait to learn more—and risk losing this opportunity**

» My name is Paulo Manteiro.

If you'll let me, I can turn this community around.

If you don't take advantage of this, others will.

Hear me out.

» Can Gloria read?

Used with permission of OxFam

The Skinny on Hyperlinking

Careful planning and use of hyperlinking is what can take a ho-hum click-along linear program to a new level of interest and engagement for learners. Branching decision making can help learners see the consequences of their actions; branching answer slides help lead a learner through a better decision process; branching quiz templates can move learners around a course to the most appropriate content for them. In the case of Mission: Turfgrass (which you can view in full at http://learn-nuggets.com/portfolio/elearn/turfgrass/player.html), branching accomplishment screens allow learners to collect items for a rucksack as they successfully navigate the course sections. Note that the learner isn't really "collecting items" but, depending on actions, is being sent to slides showing different items in the rucksack. This requires a number of branching points as well as, in some places, duplicates of slides. Setting this up requires forethought and patience as much as anything else. Kevin Thorn, an artist at heart, draws the original schematic by hand, while I usually go with Post-it Notes on a large table. Here is the story-board/schematic for the Mission Turfgrass course showing how it "works" As it is so detailed it's difficult to capture for print here, but take a look at Figure 7.47. The website contains a .pdf file of this image that can be resized and shows that the slides are color-coded as well as labeled.

Figure 7.47. Schematic for the "Mission Turfgrass" Course

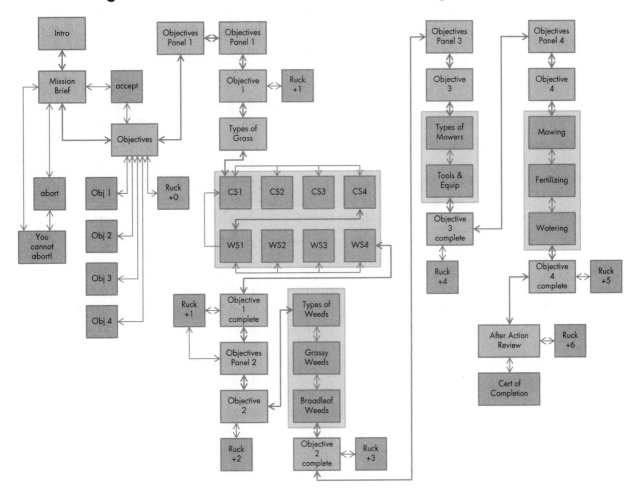

What About "Gamification"?

The advent of new technologies and the popularity of mobile devices have brought with them the concept of "gamification." It's essentially adding game elements to non-game experiences. What's important, though, is that the experience taps into a learner's intrinsic motivation and desire. It's not just adding the capability for learners to score points or earn badges. For instance, most readers by now have likely seen, if not actually played, Angry Birds. The game is built so that different levels of play are locked, and you must complete one level to advance to another. While you earn points, most players report not really caring much about that in itself. There is intrinsic satisfaction in solving the puzzle each level offers, and many players would play even if points were not offered at all.

The points in and of themselves aren't really what make a game compelling or addictive or "fun." We play because we inherently enjoy the activity. So those wanting to "gamify" their instructional activities need to look beyond timers and scoring. Apart from being enjoyable and interesting, the game needs to provide learners with many choices, with reasonable support for repeated tries, and with satisfaction from succeeding. A Jeopardy-style quiz on unlawful harassment might be more engaging than just reading a document about it, but it really isn't "gamified" as the industry currently defines it.

> One of the biggest challenges that gamification faces is the lack of understanding of what it actually is. Gamification IS NOT the use of games in a learning environment. Gamification IS NOT the same as a serious game. Gamification IS the use of game mechanics (leaderboards, badges, levels, etc.) to provide a richer experience that promotes better engagement and retention for the participant(s). This is not, however, as simple as adding badges and a leaderboard to an experience. Very serious design and thought need to be applied to the introduction and integration of game mechanics into any program. Without the work of an experienced and knowledgeable designer, gamification efforts become an exercise in frustration and futility to the users.
>
> **–Kris Rockwell, CEO, Hybrid Learning Systems,**
> **www.hybrid-learning.com**

Mazes

One last interesting interaction is the maze, created by assigning mouseover action settings to images on a slide. Mazes can be used for problem solving, decision making, or teaching sequence and process. The one shown in the figures below, ideally suited to mouse or keypad training for new computer users or tasks involving similar motion, is reminiscent of the battery-operated child's game of "Operation," in which touching tweezers to metal parts of the "body" causes a buzzer to sound. The example shown in Figures 7.48 and 7.49 was created by assigning the "collapse" animation to each girder; if touched by the cursor, the pile falls. *Note:* This example is intended to illustrate another of the many possibilities PowerPoint offers to a creative designer. No malice is intended toward kittens!

Figure 7.48. Girders Collapse If Learner Touches with Cursor

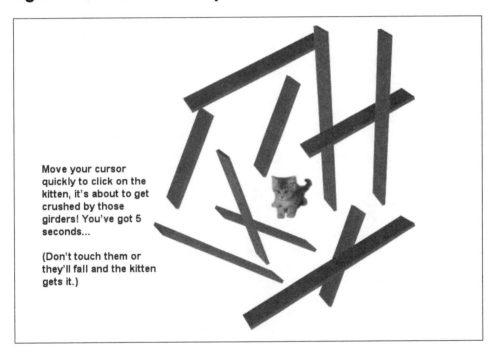

From an online PowerPoint manual available at www.agsci.utas.edu.au/ppmultime dia/. Authored by Nicholas D'Alessandro, Simon James, Anna McEldowney, and Ruth Osborne, University of Tasmania. Copyright notice: Commonwealth of Australia. Copyright Regulations 1969. This material has been reproduced and communicated to you by or on behalf of the University of Tasmania pursuant to Part VB of the Copyright Act 1968 (the Act). The material in this communication may be subject to copyright under the Act. Any further reproduction or communication of this material by you may be the subject of copyright protection under the Act.

Figure 7.49. Girders Are set to Collapse on Mouseover

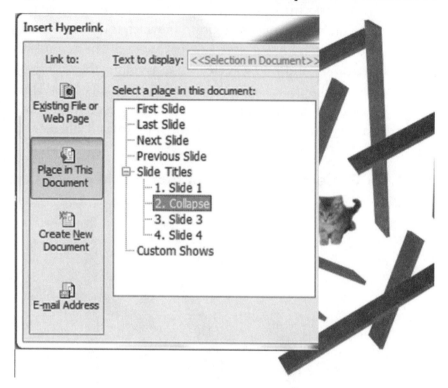

From an online PowerPoint manual available at www.agsci.utas.edu.au/ ppmultimedia/. Authored by Nicholas D'Alessandro, Simon James, Anna McEldowney, and Ruth Osborne, University of Tasmania. Copyright notice: Commonwealth of Australia. Copyright Regulations 1969. This material has been reproduced and communicated to you by or on behalf of the University of Tasmania pursuant to Part VB of the Copyright Act 1968 (the Act). The material in this communication may be subject to copyright under the Act. Any further reproduction or communication of this material by you may be the subject of copyright protection under the Act.

Treasure Hunts

Training on tasks involving research—using the company intranet, procedures manuals, or other guidelines—can be enhanced through a "treasure hunt" or "scavenger hunt" activity. Learners are assigned problems that require them to use these resources. The example in Figure 7.50 was created by a pharmaceutical company. Callers interested in purchasing prescription drugs online knew more about the process than the employees manning the company's hotline. The activity, a single PowerPoint screen with hyperlinks, helped familiarize staff with the same information being accessed.

Figure 7.50. Treasure Hunt

Treasure Hunt   **Topic: Internet Sales of Prescription Drugs**

Clue # 1	Clue # 2
Go to our page FAQs about purchasing prescription drugs online What are the three most important things to Keep in mind when counseling callers on this issue? Where else can callers find information on Purchasing prescription drugs online?	Click here to go to the US Department of Commerce What are the rules for importing prescription Drugs from outside the U.S.? What is the ONE thing we must ALWAYS caution consumers about?

Source: Bozarth, J. (2005). *e-Learning Solutions on a Shoestring: Help for the Chronically Underfunded Trainer.*

About Visual Basic for Applications (VBA)

Visual Basic for Applications is a rich programming language used by PowerPoint. With it you can create macros, which are auto-run commands for repetitive tasks. (The rolling die used in the "Bacteriopoly" game shown in Figure 7.28 uses macros; one handles the rolling die. You can see the program in full at (http://ferl.becta.org.uk/display. cfm?resID=11804). Learner machines need to have macros enabled in order to run programs that use them. VBA also allows for creation of "mini-applications." While I recommend using an external product for managing test scores, you can, with VBA, set up a self-scoring quiz entirely within PowerPoint. VBA is however, quite challenging to learn—especially for those with no other experience with programming languages or working with code—and is beyond the realm of what most typical PowerPoint users would be interested in using. For the trouble it would take to develop skill at the coding required for VBA, particularly with the goal of distributing programs as e-learning products, you could buy and learn another more robust product.

If VBA really interests you, I recommend David Marcovitz's 2004 book *Powerful PowerPoint for Educators: Using Visual Basic for Applications to Make PowerPoint Interactive*. While it focuses largely on VBA for classroom use, it is really the only book, at this time, specifically aimed at using VBA for educational applications. The book's companion website is a good resource and offers a number of examples of the types of interactions you can create with VBA: www.loyola.edu/edudept/ PowerfulPowerPoint/.

To access Visual Basic in Powerpoint 2013, click File> Options> Customize Ribbon. Under Customize Ribbon choose > Developer.

In the Code group click > Developer> Visual Basic . Look for the Visual Basic Icon shown in Figure 7.51.

Figure 7.51. Visual Basic Icon Found Under the Developer Tab

Next Stop: Add-Ons, Blending, Performance Support, and Job Aids

One of the best, yet most underutilized, capabilities of PowerPoint is that of hyperlinking/action settings. From creating interesting quizzes that offer realistic practice, to making content more interesting through the use of games, to providing simulations supplemented with audio and even video clips, PowerPoint offers the creative designer wonderful tools for creating interactivity. There is far more than just clicking "next."

So far we've discussed using PowerPoint to create asynchronous stand-alone programs. Chapter 9 offers some suggestions for blending your PowerPoint-based e-learning courses with other experiences and provides information about a low-cost tool that will let you add animated talking characters to your programs.

Add-Ons, Blending, Performance Support, and Job Aids

t's easy to extend your PowerPoint-based e-learning program. This chapter explores add-in tools, design tricks, job aids, and other ways of making your program more robust and providing additional support for your learners.

Other Documents

A common problem with PowerPoint-based shows is that the designers try to use PowerPoint to display documents that just don't fit the PowerPoint screen. Use the "Insert—Hyperlink" command to link to other files such as Word or Excel documents, or larger files such as manuals and troubleshooting guides. This will give the learners some control as well as allow the documents to be viewed as they were really intended. Links can also be used to give learners access to printable training handouts. See Figure 8.1 for an example.

Figure 8.1. Hyperlink to Other Documents

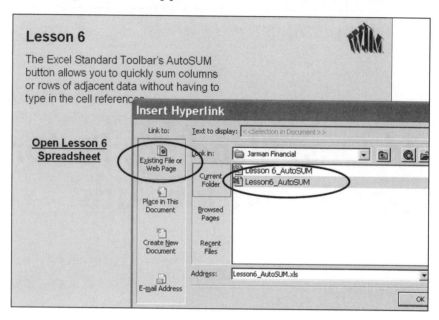

Site Samplers

A struggle in designing any training, online or otherwise, is paring the content down to the critical "must know" and culling out the "nice to know." Distilling a program to its essential elements is crucial to the success of an e-learning program, but the ruthless editing demanded results in difficult choices. Site samplers, aka "hotlists" provide a free, easy-to-build mechanism for giving learners access to the nice-to-know content. They also provide a good way for learners who want to know more to access additional information. Site samplers can easily be created by adding hyperlinks to slides. Figure 8.2 shows a site sampler placed at the end of an online program on project management:

Figure 8.2. Example of a Site Sampler

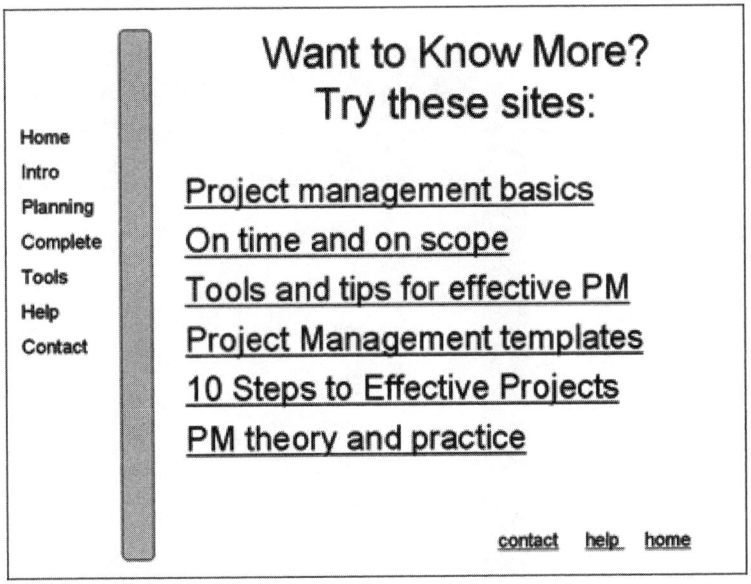

Add-On Software

SnagIt

While I am hesitant to make endorsements, there is an add-on product that really will make life easier for the designer or trainer seeking to create e-learning with PowerPoint, and at the time this book goes to press, there really is no competition for it. SnagIt, from www.techsmith.com, is intended primarily as a screen capture tool, from which you can take a shot of your entire desktop or an item on it. Virtually every image in this book, and the images used to create them (for instance, pieces of art placed on a sample PowerPoint slide) was created by capturing it with SnagIt. A one-click command brings up a small crosshair tool, which you can click and drag to select the area you wish to capture. While PowerPoint provides a basic "Insert Screenshot" command that will let you capture all or part of a screen, SnagIt provides tools for editing captured images, such as cropping, adding borders and text, removing sections of the shot, recoloring portions of the shot, highlighting areas, etc. Figure 8.3 shows a capture of the image from Figure 8.1 (reduced for the illustration here).

Figure 8.3. SnagIt Offers Options for Editing Screen Captures

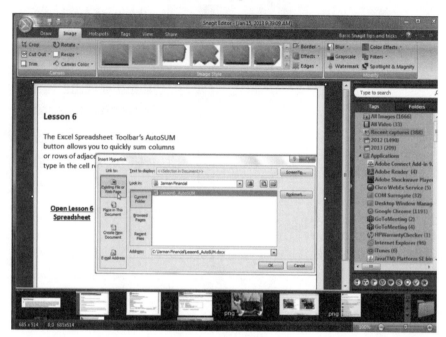

The SnagIt tools appear across the top and down the sides of the captured image. At the time this book goes to press, SnagIt sells for US $50. SnagIt additionally allows for recording of desktop animations, such as a simple narrated tutorial, although there are limitations on length of these captures and there are no editing capabilities.

The Template Issue

On the one hand, I am not a fan of what tend to be known as "templates." They're beautiful, but most were developed as backgrounds for classroom or conference-room presentations, not e-learning purposes. Figure 8.4 shows the problems that can come with presentation templates for e-learning: sidebars and other elements can eat up screen real estate and offer only decorative images, doing nothing to add to the instruction.

Figure 8.4. Template Elements Take Up Nearly Half of Slide Space

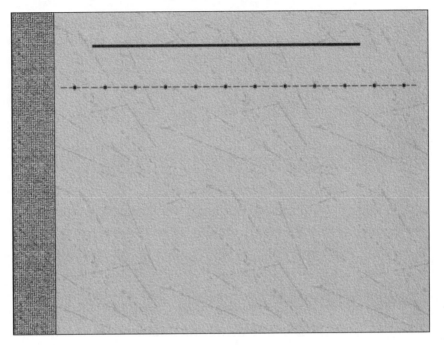

On the other hand, as discussed in Chapter 3, you probably want to create a consistent look and feel for your program. Creating your own GUI is essentially designing your own "template" and, generally, your program will be enhanced more by doing it yourself than by trying to fit your program into someone else's presentation template. The examples in Chapter 3 should have given you some ideas about this. For inspiration, though, do take a look at the thousands—really, thousands—of free PowerPoint templates available on the web. Search for "free PowerPoint templates" and their close relation, "PowerPoint backgrounds." Two good sources of these are Geetesh Bajaj's www.indezine .com and the Microsoft site www.brainybetty.com.

Other Add-Ons

 A search for "PowerPoint add-ons" will give you an idea of the array of products available. Apart from sites offering templates, there are many resources for timers, video clips, music clips, and sound effects. You'll also find designers able to help you bring complicated ideas to life and, perhaps more than anything else, you will find new ideas and approaches.

"Blending"

While "e-learning" is often used synonymously with "asynchronous" or "stand-alone," it can also be used in conjunction with other methods—particularly on the job and in the virtual or traditional classroom—for a more robust instructional experience. The virtual classroom provides an excellent bridge between the standalone and traditional classroom worlds; products such as WebEx (www.webex.com) provide extensive functionality for learners to participate via verbal discussion, written chat, whiteboarding, group activities, and even in private group break-out rooms. If you have not yet had experience with interactive synchronous training (this is distinct from "webinars," in which participants just listen to an online presenter), Jennifer Hofmann of InSync Training offers free orientation sessions. Visit her at www.insynctraining.com.

While I would argue that there is nothing that happens in a classroom that cannot be replicated online, particularly in the age of robust virtual classroom products, many instructors and learners still want some "face time" for skill practice, role play, and group discussion activities. Should you want to blend your PowerPoint-based e-learning programs with traditional classroom activities, take a look at the best qualities of both approaches. Use the "live" classroom for social tasks that are difficult (but, again, not impossible) to re-create online.

"Blending" means more than just classroom activities, however. Pre- and post-reading assignments can supplement the e-learning program and sometimes make more sense than trying to adapt the material to screens of content. (As noted earlier: If your e-learning program can be printed out as a Word document—then it should be.) Additional opportunities for "blending" your e-learning programs include add-on collaborative experiences through the use of wikis, blogs, discussion boards, and other social tools. Email also provides opportunities for learner interaction via team assignments and relay games.

Performance Support, Job Aids, and the Nice to Know

An increasingly important distinction for trainers and instructional designers is clarifying the difference between the learner having to *memorize* information versus having to *find* it. A great deal of training time (and money) is spent on providing learners with information they don't need to commit to memory. Performance of one-time procedures, rarely used skills, and multi-step processes can often be enhanced and eased by the use of job aids. This chapter offers some ideas for providing aids outside of a "training" situation.

There are also some challenges in dealing with nice-to-know, rather than must-know information. This is often lost through the culling and distilling process necessary in creating on-target e-learning programs. This chapter also includes some ideas for PowerPoint-based reference and "background" tools.

You can memorize your way out of a labyrinth if it is simple enough and you have the time and urge to escape. . . but the learning is of no use for the next time, when the exit will be differently placed.

David Hawkins

One-Time Tasks

Figure 8.5 shows an example of a screen from a new-hire orientation program. Learners are provided with blank forms as animated help notes pop up to walk them through instructions of filling out each one.

Figure 8.5. Animated Help Notes Walk Learners Through Filling Out Form

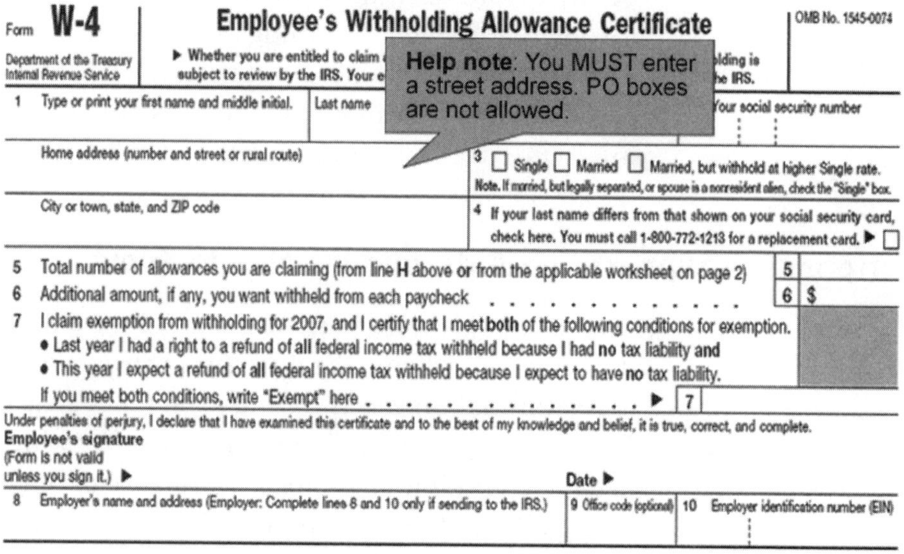

Form **W-4** Department of the Treasury Internal Revenue Service

Employee's Withholding Allowance Certificate

OMB No. 1545-0074

▶ Whether you are entitled to claim ... subject to review by the IRS. Your e... ...lding is ...he IRS.

1 Type or print your first name and middle initial. | Last name | Your social security number

Home address (number and street or rural route)

3 ☐ Single ☐ Married ☐ Married, but withhold at higher Single rate.
Note. If married, but legally separated, or spouse is a nonresident alien, check the "Single" box.

City or town, state, and ZIP code

4 If your last name differs from that shown on your social security card, check here. You must call 1-800-772-1213 for a replacement card. ▶ ☐

5 Total number of allowances you are claiming (from line H above or from the applicable worksheet on page 2) 5

6 Additional amount, if any, you want withheld from each paycheck . . . . 6 $

7 I claim exemption from withholding for 2007, and I certify that I meet **both** of the following conditions for exemption.
- Last year I had a right to a refund of **all** federal income tax withheld because I had **no** tax liability **and**
- This year I expect a refund of **all** federal income tax withheld because I expect to have **no** tax liability.

If you meet both conditions, write "Exempt" here . . . . ▶ 7

Under penalties of perjury, I declare that I have examined this certificate and to the best of my knowledge and belief, it is true, correct, and complete.
Employee's signature
(Form is not valid unless you sign it.) ▶ Date ▶

8 Employer's name and address (Employer: Complete lines 8 and 10 only if sending to the IRS.) | 9 Office code (optional) | 10 Employer identification number (EIN)

It's no secret that many workers spend a good deal of their time looking for things. One of the challenges with support tools is storing and naming them for easy retrieval. Work with your organization to clarify naming conventions and to streamline the steps a worker must go through to find a tool.

Sometime Tasks/Reference

Figure 8.6 shows an interactive table of the elements. This offers a quick overview of the chart, with user options for delving more deeply. Each item is covered with a separate transparent rectangle set to hyperlink to the corresponding explanatory slide. The explanatory slides, in turn, provide hyperlinks to external websites offering still more detail. The full program can be accessed at www.internet4classrooms.com/periodic_table.ppt.

Figure 8.6. Interactive Periodic Table of the Elements

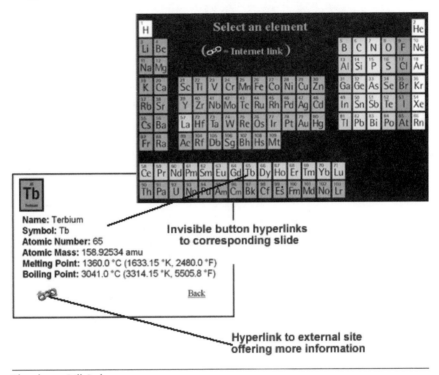

Thanks to Bill Byles

In developing job aids, consider: Where is there a great deal of rework? Where do the most questions arise, or the most mistakes occur? What's the "Hey, Joe" factor? Why do people stick their heads out into the hallway and call out "Hey, Joe! Can you show me how to. . .?" "Can you tell me again about. . .?" "I don't remember how this. . . "? If you're transforming an existing classroom course to an online format, what information would work better as support tool than "presentation"? And what information is nice to know, but not critical to performance, and might better reside outside of training?

Figure 8.7 shows a screen from animated, narrated tutorials provided to employees when a company's new phone system was installed. It gives

Figure 8.7. Telephone Tutorial

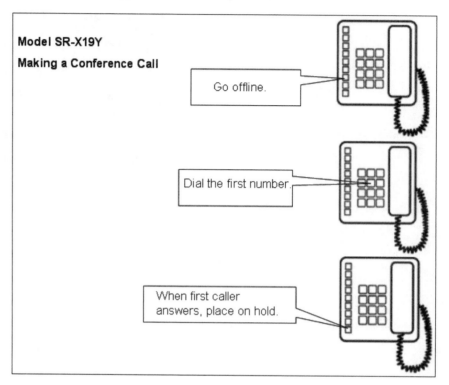

phone users access to quick help for operations they may perform only occasionally. Figures 8.8 through 8.11 show other tutorials for employees in a new-hire program. The last few years have made quick publishing of these kinds of items much easier: Create a quick tutorial in PowerPoint, save it as a video, upload it to YouTube or Vimeo, and store it as part of a library of reference tools for staff.

Locators

Figure 8.8. Interactive Map

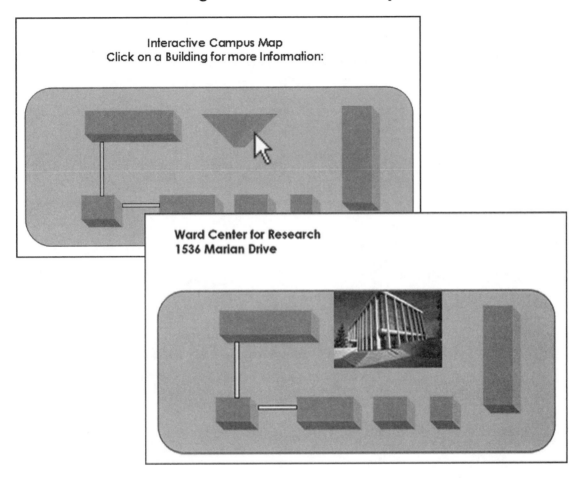

History and Background Information

Figure 8.9. Company History

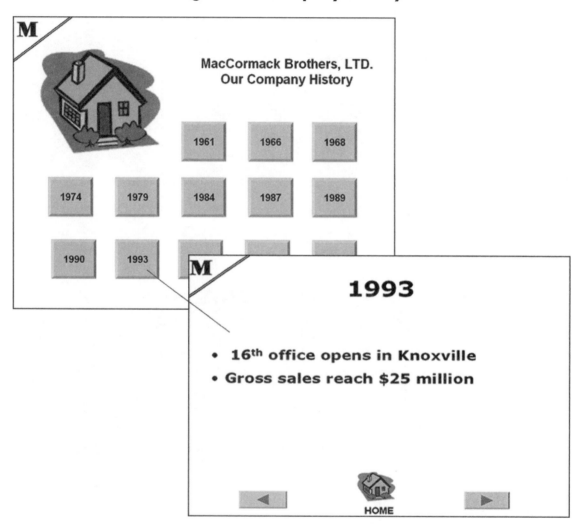

Organization Charts and Company Directories

Figure 8.10. Organization Chart

Company Policies and Manuals

Figure 8.11. From PowerPoint-Based New-Hire Orientation Program

Prompters of Process

PowerPoint's drawing tools can make it easy to create diagrams of processes. The template in Figure 8.12 could be used as either an online product or as a printable document.

Figure 8.12. Process Map Created with PowerPoint Art Tools

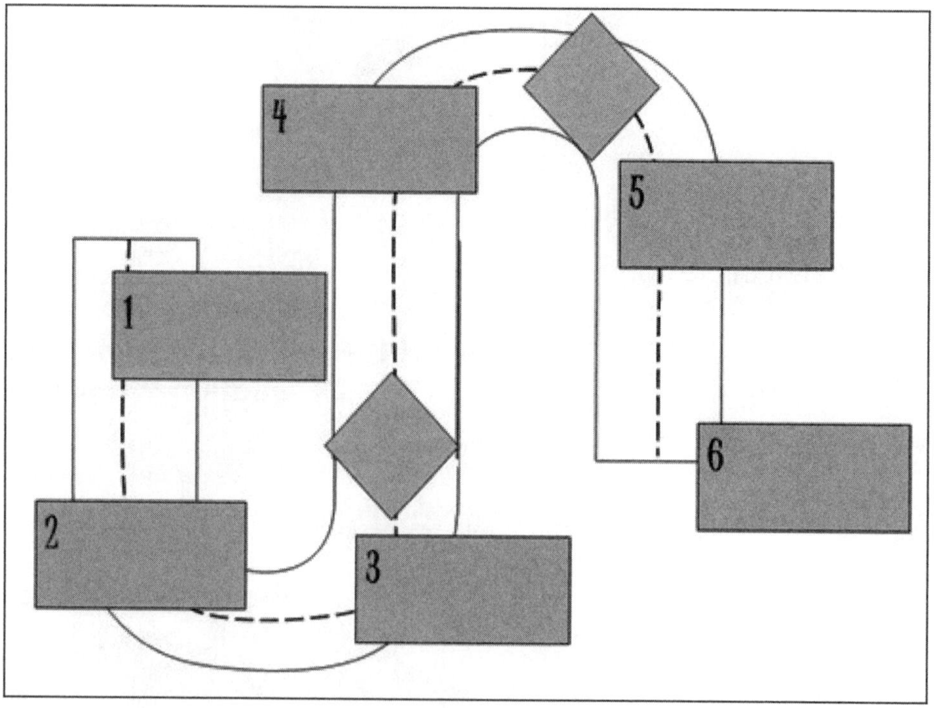

One challenge with job aids is making sure they're accessible: learners have to be able to find them. Figure 8.13 shows a desktop setup for a new hire's first day. The "Help" section contains quick tutorials on using office equipment, an interactive company map, and links to policies, forms, and other documents.

Figure 8.13. New Hire's First Day

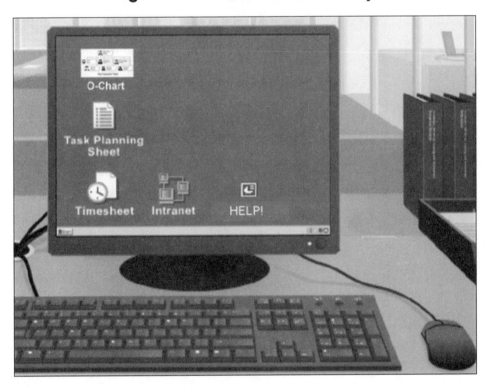

Next Stop: Adding Narration and Multimedia

The idea of creating e-learning with PowerPoint isn't necessarily confined to PowerPoint slides. Linking to external sites and documents, blending the e-learning course with live classroom events, and involving learners in online collaborative activities can all shore up the effectiveness and extend the reach of your e-learning program. Good job aids can help link training—e-learning, classroom, or otherwise—back to on-the-job performance. The thoughtful use of an animated character can add appeal and a "human" touch as well.

The next chapter brings us to the final stage in e-learning program development: adding narration and multimedia elements.

Adding Narration and Multimedia

he last step in development of your e-learning program is adding narration and sound effects. Waiting until other development is completed will save time and effort, and perhaps money, as narration will only have to be recorded once. This chapter covers ways of adding narration and other multimedia, such as sound effects, video, and Flash objects, to your PowerPoint-based e-learning program.

 See the website for tutorials on adding narration, sounds, and video.

Adding Narration

By far the bulk of the "What do you think?" calls I receive about e-learning design are on the issue of narrating PowerPoint. Most often the calls come because someone has discovered a software product that he or she believes will "let" him or her add narration. This capability is already built into PowerPoint and is a simple few-clicks proposition. I am providing some detailed directions here as the prospect of adding narration seems so daunting for many PowerPoint users. (And I can't help but wonder whether the salespeople for some of these other products are making narration sound complicated and tricky.) Recording narration really is a very user-friendly process and is certainly easier than having to install and learn to use an external product.

PowerPoint 2007 and earlier included more audio functionality than more recent versions. This allowed you to choose settings that gave a nice balance between the sound quality and the file size. Newer versions, unfortunately, include only a basic version of Sound Recorder. It will allow you to record and is easy to use, but provides only a mono file and, frankly, doesn't sound very good. If you have access to an older version of Windows you may want to record your audio files there, then save and import them into your newer PowerPoint shows. There are also a number of tools, some of them free, that will allow you to record audio of better sound quality, with more options for editing. Among the most popular of these is Audacity. Some of the converter tools also offer recording and audio editing capability better than that now provided in Windows. Here are instructions for recording within PowerPoint and for importing a file from an external source or older version of Windows.

> Remember Mayer's findings on the split attention principle: Learning is enhanced when audio is not just a word-for-word repeat of on-screen text. This causes cognitive overload, as the audio and written material compete with each other for the learner's attention.

Microphones

While many computers now come with built-in microphones ("mics"), they tend to be of low audio quality and cannot be positioned. External computer mics can be purchased at computer supply and electronics stores and range in price from US $5 to hundreds of dollars. While I have an assortment of mics, several of them quite expensive, I get the best results from a $20 tabletop version I picked up at an office-supply store and a $30 headset/mic combo from Logitech from an online computer store.

Narrator

Voice quality matters to program credibility and the learner's willingness to listen. If you are working with learners in different parts of the world, be sure to use the voices that learners will find most relevant to their day-to-day work settings. Your audience's needs are important here, even if it means recording English narration separately with British, Australian, and American voices. Also, it's worth the effort to find a narrator with a clear, pleasing voice. Check the phone book for local acting or broadcasting schools or talent agencies, and look online for companies that provide voice talent on a per-project basis. I am fortunate to have a co-worker, a former radio station disc jockey, who happily lends us his "golden tones" from time to time. Provide your narrator with a legible script, and try to reduce the number of pages you ask him or her to handle at one time, as mics will pick up the rattling of pages.

Lesson Learned

Before bringing in the narrator, read the text aloud yourself. You will likely be surprised at how wordy your script sounds and how long the script takes to read. Go back and edit—ruthlessly—before recording.

Location

While you can spend plenty of money on building or renting a sound-proof recording room, in truth you can probably get by with any space in which you can reduce echoes and outside noise. A small closet or storage room with walls lined with carpet remnants will do just fine, and failing that, a closet filled with clothes can make a passable "studio." Be sure to close windows and remove anything that creates ambient noise, like printers, and cut off air conditioning units. You may also need to place the computer itself outside of the recording space so the mic doesn't pick up the sound of the computer fan running. If you're using a makeshift studio, like a home closet, be sure to provide your narrator with a lamp.

> The personalization effect is that students learn more deeply from a multimedia explanation when the words are presented in conversational style rather than formal style.
>
> **Richard Mayer,** *The Promise of Multimedia Learning*

Recording Voice: Step by Step

There is a "narration" tutorial on the website accompanying this book, but as this seems to be task of particular interest, I am also providing basic instructions here.

First, click "Slide Show—Record Slide Show," as shown in Figure 9.1, and check whether you wish to start recording on the first or some subsequent slide. Figure 9.2 shows the steps start-to-finish.

Figure 9.1. Click "Slide Show—Record Slide Show"

Figure 9.2. Steps for Recording the Show

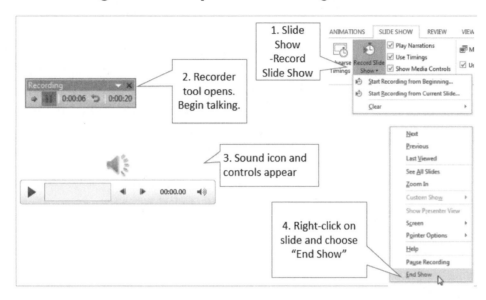

Recording Narration: Another Option

The Sound Editor tool included with Windows versions prior to 2007, and accompanying sound settings in earlier versions of PowerPoint, allowed for creation of higher-quality files and more detailed control over editing. It is unfortunate that this capability was removed, as I found it very useful. Solutions for creating higher-quality sound exist with a number of good external sound editors. The most popular is Audacity, although other good tools exist. These allow for much more editing control and more precise timing. Some converter tools, like those mentioned in Chapter 10, include audio tools as well. Each tool will offer instruction on adding the narration to slides.

Adding Sound Effects and Music

Figure 9.3 shows a slide (from the "challenging caller" simulation first shown in Chapter 7) with two sound effects. When the slide loads, learners hear a ringing phone, then are asked to click on that phone to hear comments from an angry caller. The ringing phone sound effect was downloaded from an online clipart service and saved in my files. It was inserted via the command "Insert—Audio—Audio on my PC" and is set to play when the slide loads. The angry caller's voice was recorded with the Sound Recorder. To play the voice clip, an action setting was assigned to the photo of the phone. When the learner clicks on the photo, the voice clip will play. Figures 9.3 through 9.5 provide an overview of creating the slide.

 A working example and instructions for creating this "angry caller" example are included on the website.

Figure 9.3. Slide Contains Two Sounds: Ringing Phone and Caller's Voice

That's Mrs. Jeffers now.

Click on the phone to hear what she has to say.

Click "Esc" to exit this example.

Let's look first at how to create the ringing phone. It's inserted ("Insert—Audio—Audio from my PC") from the file where I saved it, in this case my own clipart gallery. I rerecorded this single sound so that the phone would ring three times. Note that once the sound is inserted a small horn icon and controls will appear on the screen. I use the options to set the sound to play automatically. Then I hide the icon and player (Figure 9.4).

Figure 9.4. Insert Ringing Phone Sound, Hide the Sound Icon/Control, and Set the Ringing Sound "Automatic"

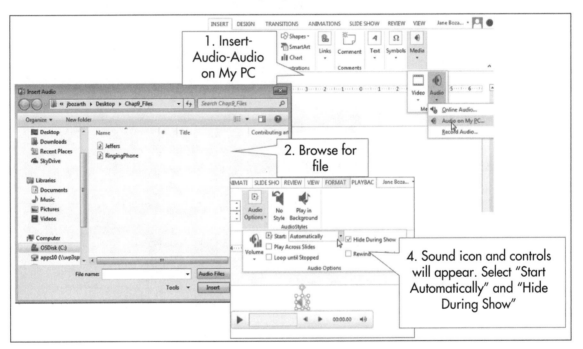

Now let's look at the second sound, the voice clip from the angry caller Mrs. Jeffers, which was recorded in PowerPoint. This sound is learner-activated, so we need to select the photo of the phone and give it an action setting ("Insert—Links—Action"). Choose "mouse click" and browse for the voice clip, as shown in Figure 9.5.

Figure 9.5. Set Audio Clip to Play When Phone Is Clicked

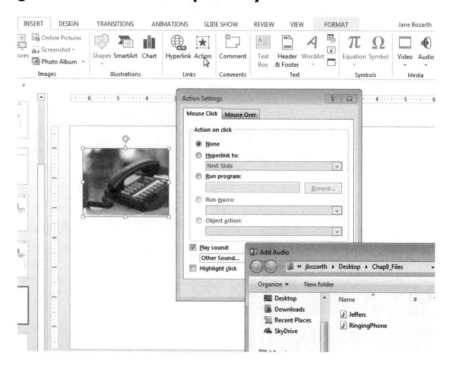

Open the slide in slide show mode. The phone will ring three times. Click on it to hear the customer's voice.

Recording Sounds—Another Option

As with the "Slide Show—Record Slide Show" function, PowerPoint also provides a tool for recording sound effects. You can access this via "Insert—Media—Audio—Record Audio" (as shown in Figure 9.6).

Figure 9.6. Accessing the "Record Sound" Tool

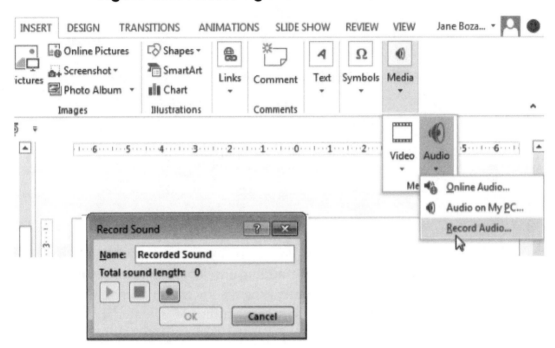

Adding Music

The process for inserting music is the same as with any other sound: "Insert—Media—Audio." As with sound effects, you can choose when the sound will play and whether it will repeat. When you insert the file the same moveable, resizable horn icon and controls will appear on the slide. Use the Effects Options tool to choose specifics about how the music will play.

Copyright

When using music and sounds in your program, be sure you have copyright clearance before using any audio files intended for "public performance," including e-learning as well as classroom applications. Even music and sound effects offered online as "royalty free" still come at a fee for use, just not on a per-play basis, as is the case with, for example, songs played by radio stations. Write the copyright holder for permission to use music, or subscribe to one of the many online clipart services that also offer music files.

Adding Video

Adding video to PowerPoint is really quite easy and can be a very effective way of, for instance, adding a welcome from your CEO or commentary from a subject-matter expert, showing an overview the workings of a piece of machinery, or incorporating video material created in another program, such as an Excel tutorial captured with Camtasia or SnagIt.

 See the website for instructions on adding video; these use an example from an Excel tutorial.

Adding video is done in the same way as inserting any other media element: choose "Insert—Video," then browse for the video clip.

PowerPoint 2013 offers extended options for video formats (see Figure 9.7). As with other effects, you can set the video to play automatically when the slide opens or on a mouse click.

However, due to the large file size associated with most video clips, and the fact that some converter tools (see Chapter 10) can't handle video conversion, another and possibly best alternative is to insert a hyperlink to your video clip so that it isn't packaged within the PowerPoint file. You may find this gives better playback results as well as reducing file size. Test before launching and see which approach seems better for your program.

Figure 9.7. Insert Video Clip

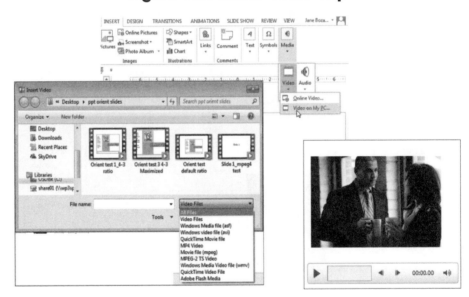

PowerPoint 2013 offers new options for working with videos, including formatting shapes, borders, sizes, and adjusting colors, as seen in Figure 9.8.

There are also new effects, shapes, and frames for videos, seen in Figure 9.9.

Figure 9.8. Video Formatting Options

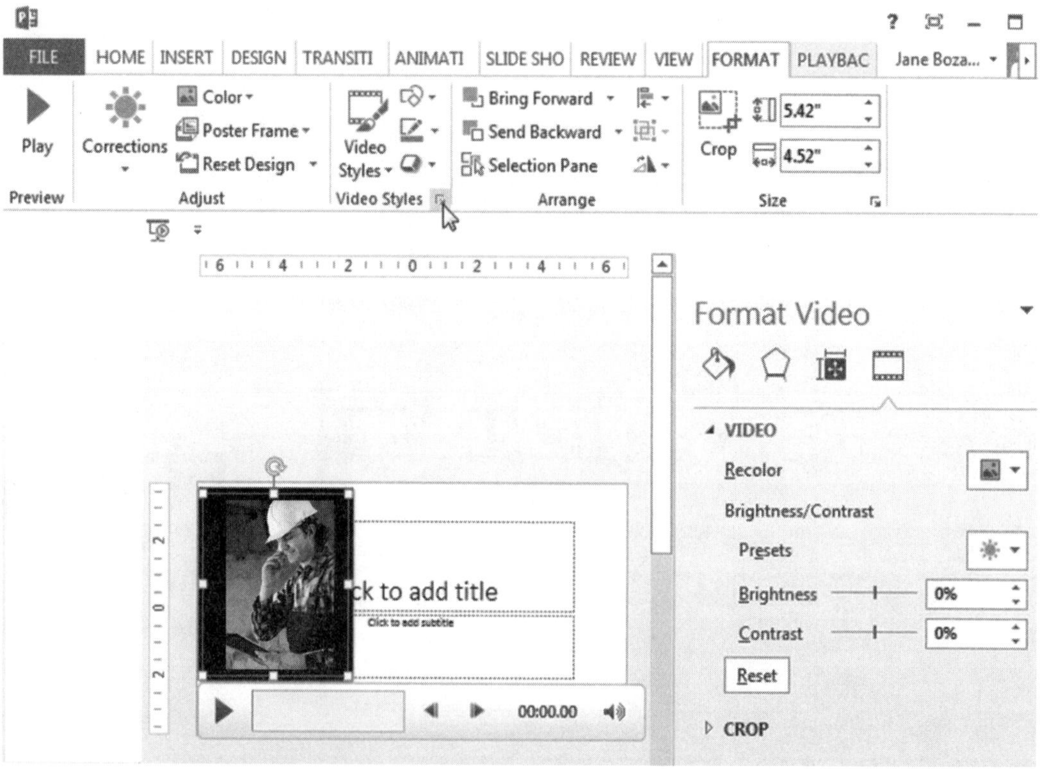

Figure 9.9. Video Effect Options

An Aside: Do You Really Need Video?

One of the most expensive undertakings related to e-learning is developing, recording, and editing custom video. This has improved with the availability of inexpensive digital video cameras and editing software, now available even on many hand-held devices. For desktop editing, Windows Movie Maker is available for free download from Microsoft. Even if you don't have to rent equipment or hire professional actors, creating custom video can be a very time-consuming undertaking. As with animation, consider: What will the video add that still photos will not? Will the motion somehow provide instruction? Several excellent programs already mentioned in this book, shown again in Figures 9.10 through 9.12, use photos rather than video without affecting the integrity or effectiveness of the instruction.

Figure 9.10. "Nail Care" Uses Photos

Read care plan and consult with resident.

Previous   Next

© Commonwealth of Australia 2006. "Nail Care" program ©
Commonwealth of Australia 2006. This product has been produced
on behalf of the national training system. It was funded under
the Australian Flexible Learning Framework administered by the
Commonwealth of Australia. This work is copyright and licensed for
Australia and New Zealand under the AEShareNet Share and Return
License (AEShareNet–S Licence). Requests and notification regarding
the use of these materials should be addressed to Training Copyright,
Department of Education, Science and Training, GPO Box 9880
Canberra City, ACT, 2601 or email copyright@training.com.au.

Figure 9.11. "Gamekeeper's Conundrum"

Source: Royal Veterinary College

Figure 9.12. Workplace Harassment

Source: www.Brightline Compliance

Next Stop: Saving, Uploading, and Distributing Your Program

Well-considered narration and other multimedia effects can greatly enhance your PowerPoint-based e-learning program. Adding this material is the last stage in program development. Chapter 10 explores the end result of all your work: saving the final program and uploading it to the Internet for delivery to your learners.

Delivery and Support

Distributing Your e-Learning Program

The final step in creating e-learning with PowerPoint is to put it on the web. You may be working with your own internal information technology staff for this; if so, they will likely provide server space on which you can store your files, and may be willing to do the file upload for you. Or your IT department may assign you space on your organization's server so you can upload the files yourself. You'll need free FTP (file transfer protocol) software for this. Uploading is as simple as dragging and dropping files from your computer onto the server; just be sure to upload everything associated with the PowerPoint show, including audio clips and any external documents, like printable handouts. What and how you upload may depend partly on how you choose to save the file. See the following for more information.

You may already have invested in a learning management system (LMS) on which to host your programs. That product will offer specific guidance in how to upload materials and in what format they should be saved. Also, many converter tools now offer a one-click "publish to LMS" option that generates all the additional files needed for that process.

Or you may have neither internal IT support nor an LMS and will need to acquire your own hosting services. You will be loading your programs onto a server hosted by an external company, so will need the free FTP software mentioned above. If you're new to this kind of technology, go with a provider that will help you get started. Many now offer very user-friendly interfaces and tutorials. Also, before choosing a plan, gain an understanding of what you want to deliver and how many users you are likely to have. Large files with audio and video clips will require a good deal of server space, so you will need to think about how much storage space you'll need.

The other big issue is data transfer ("bandwidth"). This is the amount of data that is transferred from your account as learners access your e-learning programs. It's important that you have enough of both storage space and data transfer capability, so this is one time I recommend overbuying. Good news: hosting is fairly inexpensive, with most plans offering a good deal of space for less than US $10 per month. Apart from cost, when choosing a hosting service check references to find out about the company's quality, Ask around, for instance, about the frequency and duration of service outages and availability and competence of live help.

If you are only interested in running a course of fairly small size or two at a time, you might even be able to get away with using a free blogging platform like WordPress or Blogger to host the files.

About Bandwidth

There is no such thing as "unlimited" bandwidth. Some hosting companies make this promise with the (realistic) assumption that most websites will never use all that much. Running e-learning programs is an entirely different matter and something your host may not have considered.

Saving and Uploading Your Files

As I've previously mentioned, there are four ways to save your PowerPoint-based e-learning program for distribution on the web:

1. Upload as is.

2. Save it as a PowerPoint Show (.pps) file.

3. Convert it to an HTML5 or Flash (.swf) file.

4. Do it yourself and save it as a video file (MP4, WMV).

1. Upload It as Is

You can just save the file as a PowerPoint presentation (in 2013, this is a .pptx file extension) extension and email it or upload it to a website. To open the file, learners will need to access it on a computer with PowerPoint installed.

2. Save It as a PowerPoint Show (.pps) File

The file will open as a full-screen PowerPoint show that learners can open or save to their own computers. Learners will need the free PowerPoint viewer.

3. Convert It to an HTML5 or Flash (.swf) File

Saving the PowerPoint presentation as HTML5 or Flash will compress the files. For most e-learning programs created with PowerPoint, this may be the best choice. Why? Mostly because PowerPoint files, especially those with animation, narration, or music, are enormous. They can eat up bandwidth and, if saved with a .pps extension, can take a long time to open, as the entire file must load before any screen is displayed. There are a number of low-cost (less than $500, and some less than $100) software programs that will convert the PowerPoint file to a smaller Flash (this will have an .swf extension) or HTML5 file. Programs converted to one of these formats will stream more smoothly, take up less space on the server, and consume less bandwidth while running.

But there are big changes coming. In the past, converting to Flash was a safe choice: Flash files would display properly on any screen, from large monitors to small hand-held devices, and a free Flash player was nearly ubiquitous and already installed on most computers. However, with the release of the iPhone, Apple decided against supporting Flash, and the trend has caught on. At this time Flash files will not run on iPhones and similar devices without workarounds likely inconvenient for learners. And the day is coming when browsers will no longer support Flash either. Things change, and it's likely that plug-ins or players or such will evolve to allow Flash to run, but in light of all the changes this may not be the best choice for much longer.

You've probably heard of HTML, hypertext markup language, which for many years has been the standard basis for most web pages. HTML5 is the most recent version of HTML, and it makes it easier for program-mers to add rich media to websites; basically, media such as video and music can run without reliance on third-party software like Flash or QuickTime. PowerPoint-to-HTML5 converters are quickly emerging in this fairly new field. Given what is the likely future of Flash, using an HTML5 converter might be the better choice.

The good news about converters is that the products are usually very easy to use, and you don't need to purchase or know how to use Flash software or do HTML5 coding to use the converter tools. They'll also give you choices about compressing the file to make it smaller (note that this will affect quality) and can add bookmarking so the learner, if inter-rupted, can pick back up where he or she left off. Figure 10.1 shows the dashboard for the iSpring converter.

Most converter tools will let you add slide counters and set options for navigation. Be aware that if you are using hyperlinking—such as a multi-ple-choice scenario with several choices, or a branching simulation with

Figure 10.1. iSpring Pro Converter Dashboard

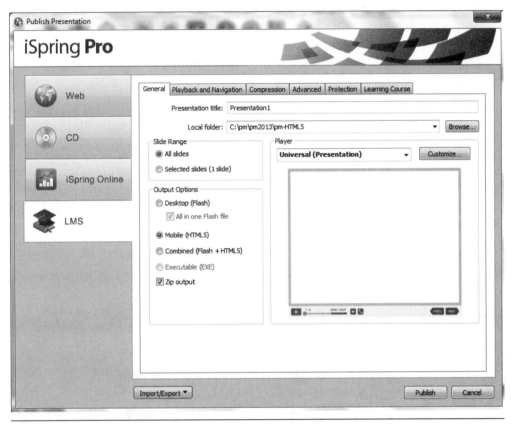

iSpring images used with permission

a number of decision points—you will want to disable any auto-navigation or buttons so that the learners can interact directly with the slides. Also, the use of such interactions add to the slide count and may make the learners think there are, say, eighty slides when, depending on their choices in the interactions, they will only actually access sixty. For this reason I usually turn off the slide counter, too.

Know your tool. While converter products are similar, each has its own quirks. Some animations are converted seamlessly by one and lost by another. Some converters automatically insert navigation buttons that can be difficult to override. Some inexplicably cost, and this is not an exaggeration—1000 percent more than others, even though the functionality and quality are the same. And remember: Before you purchase anything, you need to be fluent with PowerPoint itself, too. Costs of converter tools are often run up by the addition of "features" that replicate something PowerPoint already does. (See the text box below.) Try demos and free trial periods to see the eccentricities of the tools you're considering, and go with the one that seems to do most of what you plan to for the most reasonable price. Some popular converter tools include those offered by Conaito and HTML5Point, but take time exploring options and choosing the best tool for your needs. Also, companies such as iSpring and Articulate (www.articulate.com) offer, by way of extending their converter tools, a suite of add-on products for building quizzes and tracking completion as well as providing a "SCORM wrapper" necessary for running the file in an LMS.

Most converter tools will allow you to add (or disable) features such as an outline view. Figure 10.2 shows an example of this in Articulate.

Figure 10.2. Example of Full Player View

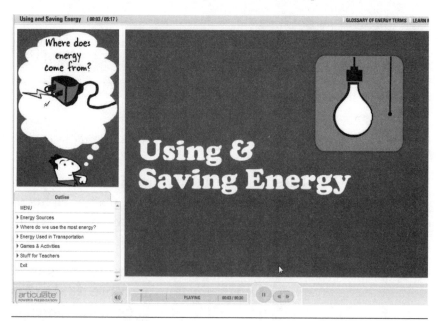

Articulate image used with permission

The Articulate example, created by Tom Kuhlmann, is also interesting for his use of that space. The small image in the presenter panel is actually a video built in PowerPoint and saved as an MP4 file. It's included on the website if you'd like to take a look.

Lesson Learned

As you finalize and prepare to distribute your materials, be sure you are working with only one final copy of the program. Trying to edit multiple versions, or to keep up with different copies from different stakeholders or reviewers, will quickly prove cumbersome and create confusion.

4. Do It Yourself; Save It as a Video (MP4, WMV) or Other Format

While you can do the conversion from PowerPoint to Flash or HTML5 "by hand," it is a rather complicated affair and might be more than you want to take on. The directions for doing the conversions can be found online (try searching for "convert PowerPoint to Flash [or HTML5] manually," but really, if you are planning to create a lot of programs with PowerPoint, investing in a converter tool might be a better choice for you. If you don't already have the Flash software, you'll need to purchase it in order to do the conversion manually.

A Recap

We've reviewed various ways to save your e-learning program and distribute it to your learners. Let me summarize the pros and cons of different file types for you:

PowerPoint 2013 offers more options for saving files, including Windows Media File and MP4 (short for MPEG-4). MP4 is an appealing option, as it will play back on almost any device. But be aware: This is a video file, and it will play like a movie. The learner will have controls for start, stop, forward, back, and volume, but there will be no learner control of the actual program. Links and navigation buttons and triggers and such will not work. This might be the right choice for something like a stand-alone AutoPlay tutorial, but it provides a very passive view-only experience for learners.

One More Option: Save as CD

While "e-learning" is most often defined as something delivered over the Internet, you do have the option of saving your programs to CD. You can save the files in several of the same ways you've seen them described for web deployment (in their original form, as PowerPoint shows, or converted to HTML5 or Flash files). The advantages: file size will be far less a consideration, and bandwidth will not be an issue at all. The disadvantage, and it's a big one: if you need to make a change or update, you must locate and replace all the existing CDs.

Content Libraries and Reusable Learning Objects

Be sure as you create materials that you store it in ways that will help you retrieve and reuse it later. Images, video clips, narration clips, GUIs, storyboards, and screenshots are all items you might have used at another time, either with a new program or an update to an existing one. If you have access to an LCMS (learning content management system), you'll likely already have protocols and clear guidelines for doing this. See the note about SCORM and shareable objects. For those storing materials in "homemade" libraries, work to develop clear naming conventions and storage places, such as a shared file on your organization's intranet, so that materials can be located.

Tracking

"Tracking" is a hot-button word in e-learning. Where for years we've "tracked" participation by having learners sign attendance sheets, suddenly in the era of e-learning we feel we need so much more technology to accomplish this. You may already own a learning management system (LMS) to which you plan to link your PowerPoint-based e-learning program. If not (and this is especially important to those of you on tight budgets), consider: What are you really trying to track, and why? What will you do with the data? Many sophisticated tracking systems produce ninety-six reports, and often none of them has exactly the information you need. Are you tracking for compliance? To protect yourself in lawsuits? Or because it's a habit? What do you really need to know?

- How many people accessed the course?

- Whether Jane accessed the course?

- Whether Jane started and finished the course?

- Whether Jane passed the test?

- Whether Jane. . . ?

- . . . and so on

PowerPoint lends itself to several fairly easy solutions here. For instance, you can:

- Include a hyperlink to a completion form that the learner can save, forward, or print and submit to an administrator, as shown in Figure 10.3.

- Include an email link to an administrator, or to a separate mailbox set up for completions by topic. An example is shown in Figure 10.4.

- Link to a hosted online form or a final exam using a tool available from an online survey or quiz engine like www.Surveymonkey.com or www.Quia.com, which can offer reporting functions similar to that of an LMS.

Figure 10.3. Printable Completion Form

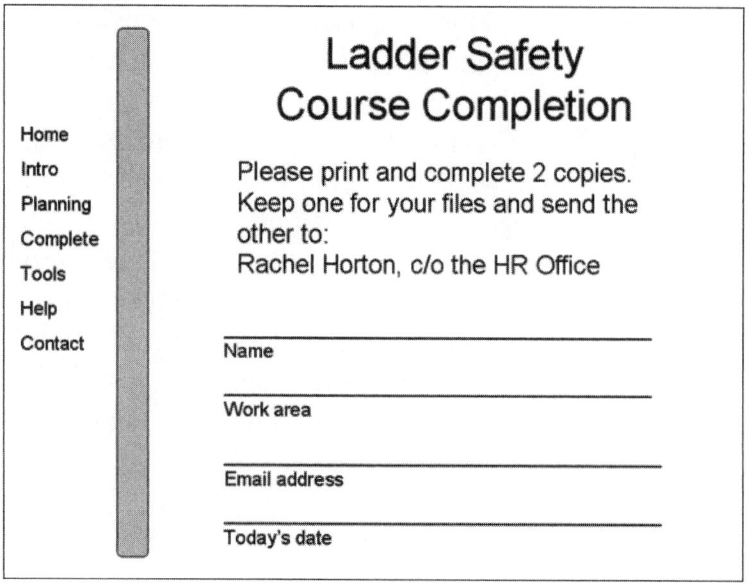

Ladder Safety
Course Completion
Home
Intro
Planning
Complete
Tools
Help
Contact
Please print and complete 2 copies. Keep one for your files and send the other to:
Rachel Horton, c/o the HR Office
Name
Work area
Email address
Today's date

Figure 10.4. Completion Set to Auto-Email

Insert Hyperlink
Link to:
Text to display: SUBMIT
ScreenTip...
Existing File or Web Page
E-mail address:
mailto:JaneLadderCourse@company.com
Place in This Document
Subject:
Course Completion
Create New Document
Recently used e-mail addresses:
E-mail Address
OK
Cancel

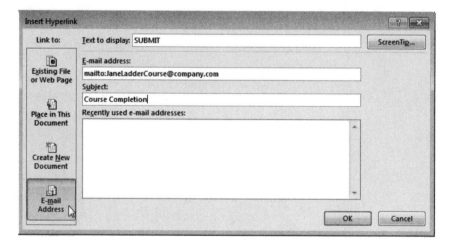

What Is SCORM and Should I Care About It?

SCORM is a term uniquely associated with e-learning and stands for "Shareable Content Object Reference Model." (While SCORM is perhaps better known, there is another standard, AICC from the Aviation Industry Computer-Based Training Committee, considered as something of an equivalent and even rival to SCORM.) It establishes standards for "interoperability," that is, standards such that different components and products can "talk" to each other. In practice it's most often used to ensure that different elements of e-learning programs or programs from assorted sources (for instance, it's not unusual for an organization to have some programs developed in-house as well as some purchased from commercial vendors) will all run on any LMS (if the organization has one). A common metaphor associated with SCORM is that of the household electrical outlet: my coffeemaker and my waffle iron both have similar plugs that fit into the wall receptacle. A "shareable content object" can be a single item, like an image or a quiz, a module from an online training program, or an entire online training program.

SCORM is only especially important if you plan to run your PowerPoint-based e-learning program on an LMS. There are many other ways to track learner data (see above), and items like job aids and performance support tools, because they don't need to be tracked, don't have to be associated with an LMS either. Even if you want your program associated with the LMS, you can just use hyperlinking to bring it in. For instance, use the PowerPoint program as is, but link to a quiz or completion form that's handled by the LMS. SCORM requires use of a programming language called JavaScript to communicate with the LMS. If you feel you need to make your PowerPoint-based e-learning programs

(*continued*)

SCORM-compliant, you can use a PowerPoint-to-HTML5 converter tool that automatically handles the SCORM compatibility (not all do, so check to be sure). Articulate Presenter is a popular converter product that includes a SCORM "wrapper," and the newer versions will output to HTML5. Or find a programmer who can help you with inserting the code.

Keeping up with tech changes is hard, and here's one more: SCORM is changing, but much later rather than sooner. SCORM is no longer being supported but is being replaced by "next-gen SCORM" for tracking more granular data, including that from activities taking place outside the LMS. At this time this is being interchangeably called the "Experience API" and "Tin Can," although that may continue to evolve. While it has seen some use from early adopters, decision making remains largely in the hands of developers still working with it. It is unclear how and when this will play out. At this time it is something not of much concern to readers of this book. Keep an ear to the ground, though, particularly if you are an LMS user.

Converter tools that publish to an LMS will likely provide you with options about the tracking standards. iSpring, for instance, provides several tracking options including one for users of BlackBoard (see Figure 10.5).

Figure 10.5. Options for Saving to a Particular Standard

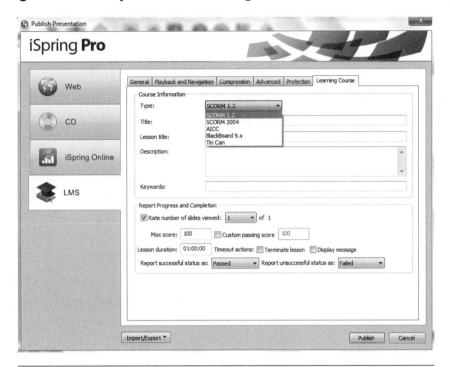

iSpring image used with permission

Test, Test, Test—and Launch!

As noted throughout this book, ongoing testing is critical to a smooth and timely program launch. I am not a proponent of the old-school "develop whole program—pilot—revise whole program" approach. It's cumbersome and can create far more rework than just "tweaking" as you go. It can also be maddeningly lengthy. One advantage of e-learning is its capacity for a quick launch and just-in-time training solutions.

As we've discussed in other chapters, you'll likely be most successful when you:

- *Develop storyboards and simple prototypes in PowerPoint.* Stakeholders—like managers, sales staff, and customers—are likely familiar with the "look" of a PowerPoint slideshow. They'll better understand the vision for the final program than if they were shown, say, a script. Obtaining clarity and stakeholder agreement early on will save time and rework later.

- *Involve end-users—your learners—up-front.* Have them try out the GUI, the Jeopardy quiz, and the external test. They can give you very useful feedback as you are creating the program. Waiting until a finished product is ready will, again, put you at the risk of rework that would have been easier if done sooner.

- *Sit and watch as your pilot users interact with the program.* Pay attention to times they seem to hesitate or are unsure about what to do/where to go next. Notice what really seems to hold their attention and what they skim or skip through. Time them to see how long the quiz really takes.

- *Test the program on different machines and browsers.* Colors display differently from one monitor to another; interactions that work just fine in Internet Explorer may inexplicably misbehave in, say, Mozilla Firefox.

Your organization may have protocols in place for launching a program. You may just be loading your files to an LMS with which your employees are familiar. I have found that an email note to learners, telling them how to access the new program and letting them know what technology they'll need (such as Firefox, the Flash player, or a printer) reduces frustration for them. The catalog that houses most of my e-learning courses has a "tech requirements" page that learners must to view before they can access any program.

If e-learning is a new endeavor for you and your organization, I'd like to add some encouraging words: I have been working with e-learning projects since 1999, in an organization with 90,000 employees from all employment categories and educational backgrounds. Despite what the literature sometimes rumors, I have experienced virtually no "learner resistance" to e-learning. Learners appreciate e-learning's just-in-time capability. They can access training when they need it, not when the training department has it scheduled. They can go back and revisit materials. They can control when and where they access the training. And they appreciate the fact that e-learning respects their time. They are not pulled from work (or, as is often the case, required to travel) to an eight-hour class that really covers only an hour or two of content. I do occasionally run into issues with employees, such as prison guards or hospital nurses, who don't have their own work computers. This has always been resolved by explaining that learners don't need their own computers, just access to one for a short while. (It's akin to explaining that an employee doesn't need his or her own photocopier.) Truthfully, though, getting access to a computer is really just a nonissue for most workers in the first world. The resistance I do encounter is more often from IT departments blocking a particular technology (usually something involving bandwidth, like video, which I can resolve by promising to launch to only a few learners at a time) and—from trainers. e-Learning is, unfortunately, perceived as a threat by some classroom trainers, who continue to fear that they'll be replaced by stand-alone online courses.

Chart 10.1. Creating e-Learning with PowerPoint

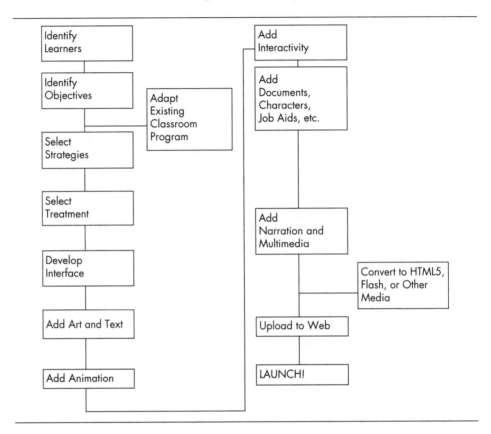

Summary

The decisions you make about distributing your PowerPoint-based e-learning program will affect decisions about design. Must you have trigger animations? If so, at least for now, you will need to deliver your program as a large PowerPoint file, likely made larger by the addition of media elements or narration. Must you limit file size? You'll either need to eliminate media and narration or deliver the program converted as an HTML5 file, which will retain the triggers. Working with your IT department, knowing the technology most widely available to your learners, will help you make good decisions about distributing your program, which in turn will help to ensure its success. The entire process is outlined in the chart above.

Author's Note

And this is the end of the book. In moving on to developing e-learning with PowerPoint, I hope you will take away the things I have tried to emphasize. e-Learning is not an objective in itself. Determine what performance issues could be resolved through training, and then choose the training solution that will solve the problem. Look beyond what we may think of as traditional training solutions. Are there job aids, documents, or activities that would solve problems? Is there a game that teaches better than a "presentation"? Technology is helping us redefine "training." Marc Rosenberg, author of *e-Learning: Strategies for Delivering Knowledge in the Digital Age*, often uses the analogy of the railroad industry's failure to adapt to the advent of trucking: the railroad industry saw itself as being in the train business, not the transportation business. As training professionals, it's likewise important that we remember that training is not about the classroom, it's about performance improvement. Learn to use tools and approaches that will help your organization achieve that goal.

And remember: good e-learning is not about software—it's about design.

PowerPoint Basics

reating e-learning with PowerPoint requires some skill at using the product. This book assumes that you have some experience with creating slide shows, including using basics of Word art, using Shapes, working with the drawing and picture toolbars, inserting and resizing clipart, and creating simple animations. A quick overview of PowerPoint tools is provided here. Experienced users may choose to just skip this Appendix; those with very rudimentary skills might want to practice basic tasks or seek out additional training. (Searching online for specific tasks, such as "how to create animations in PowerPoint," will take you to any number of tutorials.)

ON THE WEB

Keyboard shortcuts have become a bit more complex since the introduction of the "ribbon" interface. See the website for a complete list of shortcuts.

Figures A.1 through A.17 show a number of illustrations of PowerPoint commands and assorted functions.

Figure A.1. PowerPoint 2013 Interface

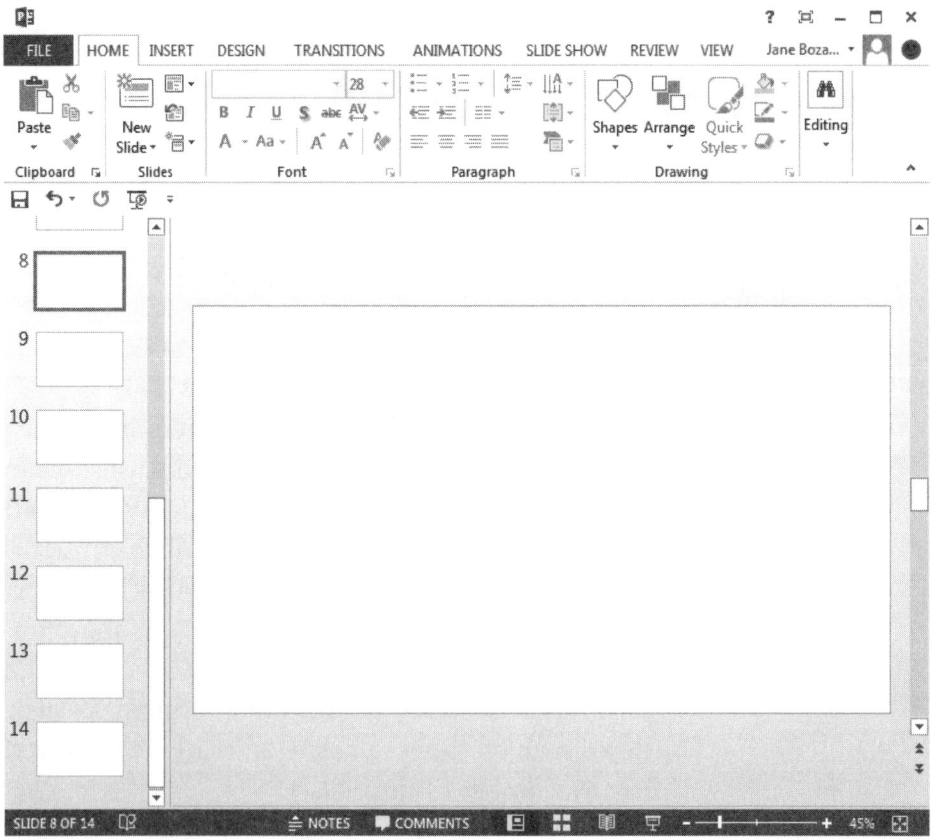

Figure A.2. "Backstage"

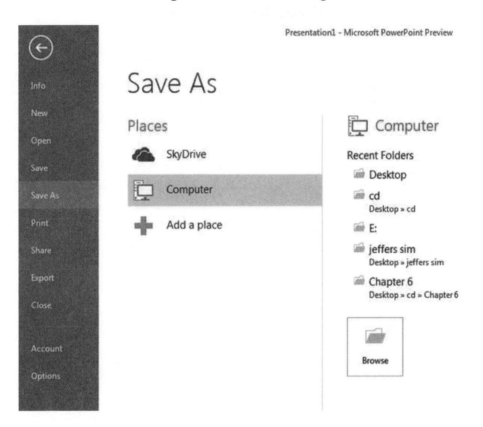

Figure A.3. Ribbon

Figure A.4. Drawing Tools (Will Open When You Insert and Highlight a Shape)

Figure A.5. Arrange Objects

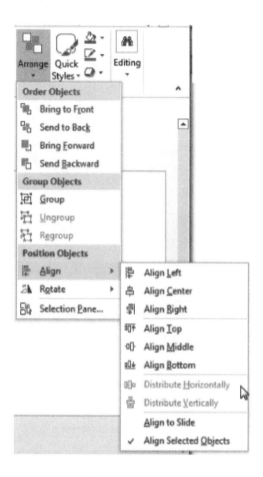

Figure A.6. Shapes

Figure A.7. Shape Effects

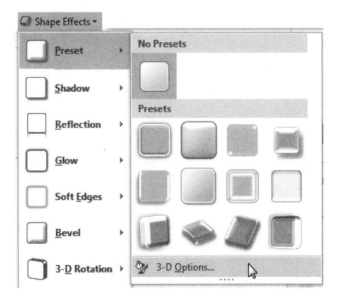

Figure A.8. Modifying Shapes

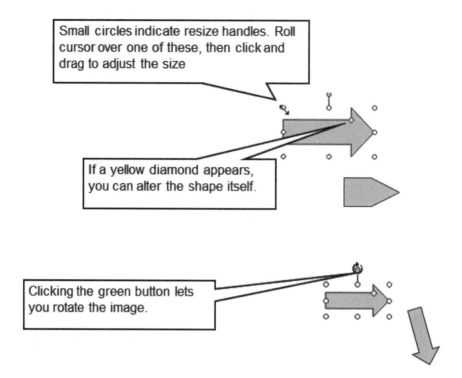

Figure A.9. WordArt Gallery

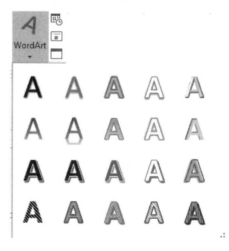

Figure A.10. SmartArt Gallery Categories

Figure A.11. SmartArt Category Example

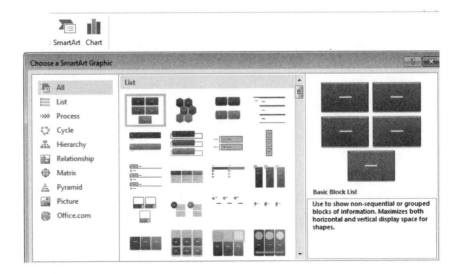

Figure A.12. Animation Tab

Figure A.13. Fill Color Palette

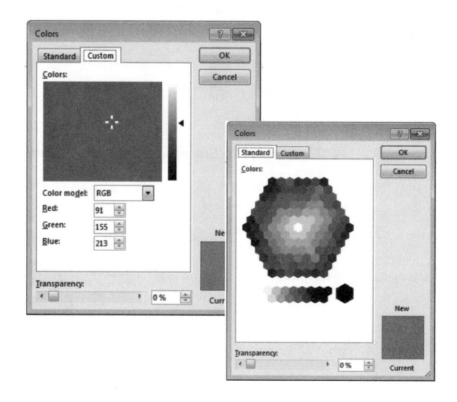

Figure A.14. Fills for Shapes

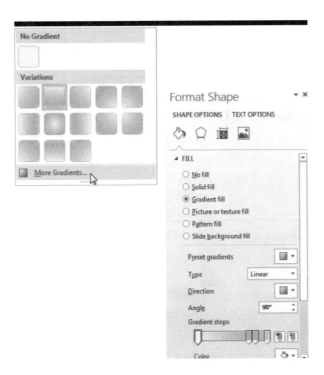

Figure A.15. About Shape Fills

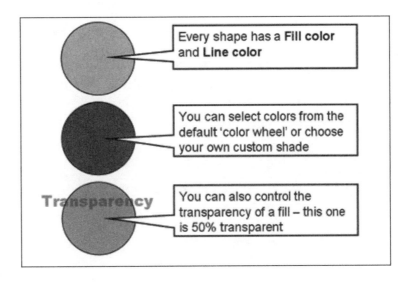

Figure A.16. Fill Effects

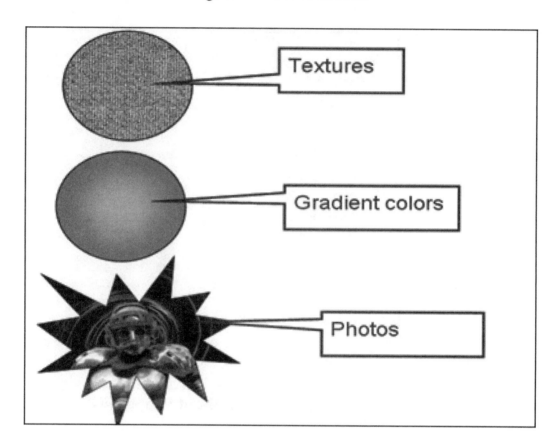

Figure A.17. Format Picture (Will Open When You Insert and Highlight a Picture)

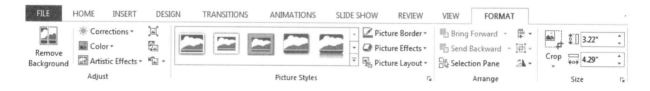

Summary

This supplement was meant to provide a quick overview of tools available in PowerPoint; familiarity with these will be helpful as you work to build e-learning programs. More sophisticated operations, such as editing clipart and recording narration, are included within their respective chapters, and many tasks are further explained on the website accompanying this book. If you are not already a skilled PowerPoint user, you are encouraged to practice and learn as much as you can. Nothing in this book is technically all that difficult, but proficiency will, of course, increase your confidence, enable your creative ideas, and reduce program development time.

REFERENCES AND OTHER SOURCES

Atkinson, C. (2005). *Beyond bullet points*. Redmond, WA: Microsoft Press.

Aust, R., & Isaacson, R. Designing and evaluating user interfaces for e-learning. Retrieved from http://elearndesign.org/papers/eLearn2005_Aust.pdf

Bozarth, J. (2005). *e-Learning solutions on a shoestring: Help for the chronically underfunded trainer*. San Francisco: Pfeiffer.

Chapman, B. (2005). *PowerPoint to e-learning development tools: Comparative analysis of 20 leading systems*. Sunnyvale, CA: Brandon Hall Research.

Clark, J. (2010). *Tapworthy: Designing great iPhone apps*. Sebastopol, CA: O'Reilly Media.

Clark, R.C., & Lyons, C. (2005). *Graphics for learning: Proven guidelines for planning, designing and evaluating visuals in training materials*. San Francisco: Pfeiffer.

Clark, R.C., Nguyen, F., & Sweller, J. (2006). *Efficiency in learning: Efficiency-based guidelines to manage cognitive load*. San Francisco: Pfeiffer.

Culberson, R. (nd). Use of characters in e-learning. Retrieved from www.nurelm.com/resources.jsp?pageId=21613922102811621475077 64

Dirksen, J. (2011). *Design for how people learn*. San Francisco: New Riders.

Fried, I. (2005, September 20). Office 12 makeover takes on "feature creep." CNET News.com. Retrieved from http://news.com.com/Office +12+makeover+takes+on+feature+creep/2100-1012_3-5873597. html?tag=html.alert

Hoober S., & Berkman, E. (2011). *Designing mobile interfaces.* Sebastopol, CA: O'Reilly Media.

Kuhlmann, T. (2007). The insider's guide to becoming a rapid e-learning pro. Articulate. Available for free download at www.articulate.com/ rapid-elearning/.

Lowe, R. (2003). Animation and learning: Selective processing of information in dynamic graphics. *Learning and Instruction, 13*(3), 157–176.

Malamed, C. (2011). *Visual language for designers.* Beverly, MA: Rockport Publishers.

Marcovitz, D. (2004). *Powerful PowerPoint for educators: Using Visual Basic for applications to make PowerPoint interactive.* Westport, CT: Libraries Unlimited.

Mayer, R. (2001). *Multimedia learning.* New York: Cambridge University Press.

Mayer, R. (2003). The promise of multimedia learning: using the same instructional design methods across different media. *Learning and Instruction, 13*(2),123–139.

Mayer, R., & Moreno, R. (2002). Animation as an aid to learning. *Educational Psychology Review, 14*(1), 87–99.

McKenzie, J. (Ed.). *From Now On: The Educational Technology Journal.* Available at http://fno.org/.

O'Day, D. (2006). Animated cell biology: a quick and easy method for making effective, high-quality teaching animations. *CBE Life Sciences Education, 5*(3), 255–263.

O'Day, D. (nd). How to make pedagogically meaningful animations for teaching and research using PowerPoint & Camtasia. Retrieved from www.techsmith.com/community/education/interview/odayanimation ipsi2006.pdf

O'Driscoll, T., & Gery, G. (2005, February). Workflow learning gets real. *Training*.

Rosenberg, M. (2000). *e-Learning: Strategies for delivering knowledge in the digital age*. New York: McGraw-Hill.

Rossett, A., & Gautier-Downes, J. (1991). *A handbook of job aids*. San Francisco: Pfeiffer.

Rossett, A., & Schafer, L. (2007). *Job aids and performance support*. San Francisco: Pfeiffer.

Silberman, M. (2005). *101 ways to make training active* (2nd ed.). San Francisco: Pfeiffer.

Schank, R. (2005). *Lessons in learning, e-learning, and training*. San Francisco: Pfeiffer.

Shank, P., & Sitze, A. (2004). *Making sense of online learning*. San Francisco: Pfeiffer.

Stolovitch, H., & Keeps, E. (2002). *Telling ain't training*. Alexandria, VA: ASTD/ISPI.

Sweller, J., van Merrienboer, J., & Paas, F. (1998). Cognitive architecture and instructional design. *Educational Psychology Review*, 10(3).

Toth, T. (2004). *Technology for trainers*. Alexandria, VA: ASTD.

Udell, C. (2012). *Learning everywhere*. Nashville, TN: RockBench.

Van Gog, T., Paas, F., & van Merrienboer, J. (2004). Process-oriented worked examples: Improving transfer performance through enhanced understanding. *Instructional Science*, 32(1–2), 83–98.

Wilson-Pauwells, L (1997). Bringing it into focus: Visual cues and their roles in developing attention. *Journal of Biomedical Communication*, 24, 12–16.

Zull, J. (2002). *The art of changing the brain*. Sterling, VA: Stylus.

OTHER RESOURCES

Several programs are mentioned repeatedly throughout this book, usually due to their particularly creative and effective approach. Most are exemplars of thoughtful design, not gee-whiz expensive technology. Readers are encouraged to visit the sites below to view these programs in their entirety:

"A. Pintura: Art Detective" from Eduweb, www.eduweb.com/pintura/

"Sexual Harassment" from Brightline Compliance, www.brightlinecompliance.com/training/preventing-workplace-harass-demo.html

"Electric Circuitry" by Simon Drane, http://ferl.becta.org.uk/display.cfm?resID=2509

"Hunger Banquet" from OxFam America, www.hungerbanquet.org

"Gamekeeper's Conundrum" and "Emergency Case Simulator," both from the Royal Veterinary College, www.rvc.ac.uk/Review/Cases/Index.htm or www.rvc.ac.uk/review/Pitfalls/pitfalls.htm

"Diversity Challenge" and "Keeping Safe," both from www.kwango.com. Examples are available on the site.

"Mission: Turfgrass" is available on the website for this book, but also see other design work from Kevin Thorn at www.nuggethead.net/

For those using PowerPoint to design e-learning, there is no single better site than the Rapid eLearning Blog www.articulate.com/rapid-elearning/ authored primarily by Articulate's Tom Kuhlmann. Also join Articulate's user community for access to hundreds of instructional videos created by customers.

Other Sources

- Ellen Finklestein: www.ellenfinklestein.com. Repository of extensive instruction and information on PowerPoint, including tricks and tips.

- Indezine.com: free PowerPoint information, templates, and backgrounds. Frequently updated; free newsletter.

- PowerPoint Heaven: http://pptheaven.mvps.org/index.html. Shawn Toh's site for glitzy, high-tech PowerPoint ideas, tricks, and tutorials. Gallery of amazing games. Free access and downloads.

- Ferl: Offers an extensive, searchable resource bank of teacher-created materials, including hundreds of PowerPoint shows. http://ferl.becta.org.uk

- Laura Bergell's www.maniactive.com site. Free templates and editable presentations.

Books, Etc.

- Finklestein, E. (2003). *How to Do Everything with Microsoft Office PowerPoint 2003*. Emeryville, CA: McGraw Hill/Osborne.

- Godin, Seth. "Really Bad PowerPoint" booklet available for free download from www.sethgodin.com/freeprize/reallybad-1.pdf.

- "What if Lincoln Had Used PowerPoint for the Gettysburg Address?" http://norvig.com/Gettysburg/

- Van Wempen, F. (2004). *PowerPoint: Advanced Presentation Techniques*. Indianapolis, IN: Wiley.

INDEX

Page references followed by *fig* indicate an illustrated figure; followed by *c* indicate a chart.

A

"A. Pintura: Art Detective": comparison of found painting to a Raphael, 197*fig*; GUI (graphic user interface) from, 56*fig*; how to use examples of, 15; *noir* movie mystery used by, 195; setting and introduction of, 195–196*fig*; story told in, 34–35*fig*. *See also* Stories/storytelling

The Accidental Trainer (Miner), 27

Acronyms glossary, 77

Action buttons: add to slide master, 68*fig*; button-based navigation, 75*fig*; hyperlinking to corresponding slides, 159*fig*; hyperlinking via, 156, 157*fig*; hyperlinking via an invisible "hotspot," 156, 160*fig*–161; PowerPoint's customizable, 57–58*fig*; preprogramming of, 58; setting, 59*fig*; ways to customize, 59*fig*. *See also* Interactivity

Add-on software: PowerPoint backgrounds, 213; PowerPoint templates, 212–213*fig*; SnagIt, 122, 211–212*fig*; WebEx for "blending," 214–215; website tutorial on PowerPoint add-ons, 214

Adding: audio clips, 54, 86*fig*, 99, 161*fig*, 225; narration, 13, 27, 226–229*fig*; sound effects and music, 225, 229–233*fig*, 234; video clips, 234–237*fig*

Advance organizer, 76*fig*

Advanced Web-Based Training Strategies (Carliner), 156

Affective learning domain, 21

AICC, 253

AIDS Program animations, 141*fig*–144*fig*

Altman, R., 128

Angry Birds game, 201–202

"Angry caller" sound effects, 230*fig*–233*fig*

Animation effects: choosing choices for setting triggers by choosing, 151*fig*; emphasis, 128, 130*fig*, 131*fig*; entrance, 128, 130*fig*, 131*fig*; exit, 128, 130*fig*, 132*fig*; motion path, 128, 132*fig*, 138–140*fig*; numbered and color coded, 130*fig*; select object and choose "Animations" to access, 129*fig*; set timings for, 133*fig*

Animations: AIDS Program, 141*fig*–144*fig*; animated line that shows smoker's path, 134*fig*; "Animation Basics" tutorial on, 127, 129*fig*–133*fig*; the basics of, 129*fig*–132*fig*; combining, 148*fig*–149*fig*; gear spin, 137*fig*; grocery bag packing, 138–140*fig*, 151; heat pump water heater, 146*fig*; help notes, 216*fig*; matching quiz, 167*fig*; mazes using, 203*fig*–204*fig*; PowerPoint used to create "reasonable facsimile" of, 148; redundancy principle application to, 27; spin animation used to illustrate turn, 138*fig*; submarine submerges, 135*fig*; telephone tutorial, 217–218*fig*; that support teaching and instruction, 9*fig*, 128–129, 133–153*fig*; trigger, 150*fig*–153*fig*, 176; working pump, 136*fig*. *See also* Visuals

Animations that teach: animated help notes to walk learners through filing out form, 216*fig*; by annotating graphics, 146*fig*; by using charts, timelines, and diagrams, 141*fig*–145*fig*; by combining animations, 148*fig*–149*fig*; Danton O'Day PowerPoint website for examples of, 140; by demonstrating how things work, 135*fig*–136*fig*; by illustrating processes, stages, or progression, 133–134*fig*; matching quiz, 167*fig*; by using mazes, 203*fig*–204*fig*; as potential PowerPoint application, 9*fig*, 128–129; practicing required to perfect creation of, 148, 149; by providing worked examples, 147*fig*–148; by showing order and sequence, 138–140*fig*; by showing realistic movement, 137*fig*–138*fig*; telephone tutorial, 217–218*fig*; by using trigger animations, 150*fig*–153*fig*

Annotating graphics, 146*fig*

Architecture: advance organizer, 76*fig*; explanation of navigation, 77*fig*; glossary of terms and acronyms, 77; sequence of slides, modules, and layout, 78; site map, 77–78*fig*. *See also* GUI (graphic user interface)

ABOUT THE AUTHOR

Jane Bozarth has been a training practitioner for more than twenty years. A graduate of the University of North Carolina at Chapel Hill, she also has an M.Ed. in training and development/technology in training and a doctorate in training and development from North Carolina State University. Jane's graduate work in online learning led to her current position as e-learning coordinator with the NC Office of State Personnel's Human Resources Development Group. Her specialty, finding low-cost ways of creating or purchasing quality e-learning solutions, led to the publication of *e-Learning Solutions on a Shoestring* in 2005 (Pfeiffer). Since then she produced the first edition of this book, *Better Than Bullet Points*, as well as *From Analysis to Evaluation* and her latest, *Social Media for Trainers*. She additionally designed *The Challenge Continues* workshop package and co-wrote *Credibility* with Jim Kouzes and Barry Posner.

Dr. Bozarth is the recipient of a LOLA award, a *Training* magazine Editor's Pick Award, NASPE's Rooney Award for innovation in government service, and an NC State University Distinguished Alumni Award. A popular conference presenter, she appears at many international industry events offering keynote, breakout, and workshop presentations.

and often appears at international events such as Nielsen Communications' Training and Online Learning Conference and Expo, the ASTD International Conference and Expo, the e-Learning Guild's online forums and many management and professional association gatherings.

Jane Bozarth and her husband, Kent Underwood, live in Durham, North Carolina, USA. She can be contacted via her website www.bozarthzone.com.